discover HOME
FREEZE DRYING

includes **TIPS, RECIPES** and **MORE!**

VOLUME 1

discover HOME FREEZE DRYING

includes TIPS, RECIPES and MORE!

VOLUME 1

Table of Contents

Table of Contents

Chapter 1
Introduction

Welcome
Your Adventure Starts Here!

You will be amazed at the versatility, ease of use, and peace of mind that your freeze dryer offers. We hope you enjoy the wonderful recipes, tips, and techniques that we've collected for you.

What Can You Do With A Freeze Dryer?

LIFESTYLE

You and your family can always have the delicious foods you love on hand and ready to eat, from quick meals for busy nights to outdoor adventures to dietary restrictions, you're covered!

FOOD STORAGE

Easily create home food storage that is tastier, healthier, and more diverse than store-bought. It will also last longer and be less expensive than store-bought food storage.

SPECIAL DIETS

Preserve food for special diets and/or specific health needs, such as lowering salt intake, avoiding allergens or preservatives, supporting vegetarian or vegan lifestyles, and more!

PET FOODS

Feeding your pets home-made freeze-dried food is a great way to keep them healthy. Freeze drying at home lets you provide food for your pets at a fraction of the cost of store-bought.

GIFTS

Freeze-dried snacks and treats make amazing gifts, and did you know you can also freeze dry herbs and botanicals? Freeze drying gives you limitless possibilities!

ALTERNATE USES

You will be amazed at some of the additional uses your freeze dryer offers. How about drying out wet papers or books, or a phone that was submerged?

History of Freeze Drying

Modern freeze drying was implemented during World War II by the U.S. as a way to keep medication for the wounded from spoiling due to uncertain refrigeration as it was being transported to war zones. The technology was refined and used extensively for use in the NASA space program, providing varieties of freeze-dried food for astronauts. In the 1980s, commercial companies began to freeze dry food using large and complicated machines. In 2014, Harvest Right introduced the world's first affordable, high-quality home freeze dryer.

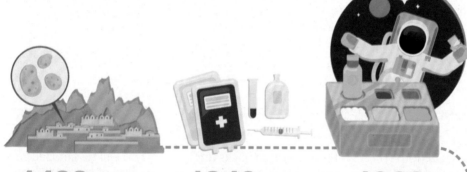

1400s
Ancient Incas froze potatoes at high altitudes in the Andes and brought them back down to villages to squeeze out liquid

1940s
Freeze drying **fully developed during World War II** to keep plasma and penicillin from spoiling

1960s
NASA uses freeze drying to **create meals for their astronauts**

1970s
US Military uses freeze drying to **improve army rations**

1980s
Commercial companies begin to freeze dry food using large, complicated freeze dryers

2014
Harvest Right introduces the first automated, high-quality freeze dryer for the home, at an affordable price

Why Freeze Drying Is the Best Method of Preservation

ADVANTAGES OF FREEZE DRIED FOOD

When food is freeze dried, it retains nearly all of its original nutrition, flavor, color, and texture. Fresh fruits, meats, and vegetables are still fresh when they are freeze dried. Cooked foods and meals are still fresh, the same as the day they were cooked. Plus, all freeze dried foods have an extraordinary shelf life, generally 10 to 25 years.

FREEZE DRYING IS THE BEST WAY TO PRESERVE YOUR FOOD FOR LONG TERM STORAGE. LEARN HOW THESE OTHER FOOD PRESERVATION METHODS FALL SHORT:

DEHYDRATED FOOD HAS A SHORTER SHELF LIFE AND DIMINISHED NUTRIENTS

DISADVANTAGES OF DEHYDRATED FOOD

The main objective with regard to food preservation is to remove moisture so that it doesn't decompose or grow bacteria and mold. Dehydrators use heat to remove about 80% of the water, whereas freeze drying in a freezing environment removes 99% of the water. Most home-dehydrated products like dried fruit, meat, and vegetables have a shelf life of one year or less. Freeze-dried food typically retains nearly all of its nutrition, whereas the nutritional value of dehydrated food is generally around 60% of the equivalent of fresh food. That's because heat used during dehydration breaks down the food's vitamins and minerals.

DISADVANTAGES OF CANNED FOOD

In order to sustain life, we need three primary things: heat, oxygen, and water. Yet these same three things also destroy our food. When food is canned, it loses important enzymes due to the high heat used in the canning process. Canning also generally changes food's texture, taste, color, and shape. Added sugar, salt, and other preservatives in canned food might also be something to avoid in many diets. Freeze-dried food retains nearly all of its nutrition, flavor, and texture.

CANNING USES HEAT WHICH ALTERS TEXTURE AND DIMINISHES NUTRIENTS

100+ Foods You Can Freeze Dry

Meals
Beef Stroganoff
Casseroles
Cheese Steak
Chicken Parmesan
Chili
Chow Mein
Enchiladas
Fajitas
Ham Fried Rice
Hash Browns
Jambalaya
Lasagna
Macaroni & Cheese
Mashed Potatoes
Meat Loaf
Meatballs
Pasta
Pizza
Roast Turkey Dinner
Roast Beef Dinner
Rice
Scrambled Eggs
Soup
Stew

Snacks & Drinks
Coffee
Cheesecake
Guacamole
Gummy Bears
Jell-O
Marshmallows
Orange Juice
Pie
Pudding
Saltwater Taffy
Salsa
Skittles
Smoothies

Herbs & Spices
Basil
Chives
Garlic
Ginger
Horseradish
Jalapeño
Lavender
Mint
Oregano
Sage
Thyme

Fruits
Apples
Apricots
Avocado
Bananas
Blueberries
Cantaloupe
Cherries
Coconut
Grapes
Jackfruit
Kiwi
Lemons
Limes
Mangoes
Oranges
Peaches
Pineapple
Raspberries
Strawberries
Watermelon

Meats
Chicken
Fish
Ham
Hamburger
Pulled Pork
Roast Beef
Sausage
Steak
Turkey
Venison

Vegetables
Asparagus
Beans
Broccoli
Carrots
Celery
Corn
Eggplant
Kale
Mushrooms
Onion
Peas
Peppers
Potatoes
Pumpkin
Spinach
Squash
Swiss Chard
Tomatoes
Yams
Zucchini

Eggs & Dairy
Cheese
Cottage Cheese
Eggnog
Eggs
Ice Cream
Milk
Sour Cream
Whipped Cream
Yogurt

How it Works

Our patented, automated technology makes it easy!

STEP 1

Fresh or cooked foods are placed on the shelves where they are frozen to -30°F or colder.

STEP 2

Once the food is frozen, the freeze dryer creates a powerful vacuum around the food. As it's slightly warmed, the ice in the food sublimates and changes directly from a solid to a gas. That water vapor is then discarded.

STEP 3

When completely dry, food is removed from the freeze dryer and sealed in moisture- and oxygen-proof packaging to ensure freshness until opened.

STEP 4

When you are ready to eat the food, simply add water. It will regain its original fresh taste, aroma, and appearance!

Foods You *Can't* Freeze Dry

A Harvest Right home freeze dryer is an amazing, versatile appliance, and most foods freeze dry beautifully.

There are only a few things that don't freeze dry well, primarily very oily foods. This is because freeze dryers extract water from food, but the oil remains. Pure butter, pure peanut butter, and pure honey as well as syrups, jams, and pure chocolate will not freeze dry. However, if these items are included in other foods, they will freeze dry just fine.

EVEN IF THEY CAN'T BE FREEZE DRIED ON THEIR OWN, WHEN THESE ITEMS ARE INCLUDED IN OTHER FOODS, THEY WILL FREEZE DRY JUST FINE!

PEANUT BUTTER

JAMS

BUTTER

HONEY & SYRUPS

CHOCOLATE

OILS

A Note About Enzymes & Bacteria

FREEZE DRYING DOES NOT DESTROY ENZYMES

Heat, commonly used in other methods of food processing such as canning and dehydration, invariably alters the structure and chemistry of the product. The advantage of freeze drying is the preservation of food's structural and chemical composition with little or no alteration. Freeze-dried foods are the closest that preserved food gets to retaining its natural composition with respect to structure and chemistry. Foods that are freeze dried are simply placed in a form of stasis until water is added back to the food. Freeze drying food removes the water without damaging the food. The water is removed in a cold environment and doesn't kill the important enzymes. Removing the water from the food halts the growth of germs and bacteria. Once the food has been freeze dried, it is placed in a container with an oxygen absorber and sealed.

With proper packaging, the food can remain in its fresh, healthy, nutritional state for 15 to 25 years or more.

FREEZE DRYING DOES NOT KILL BACTERIA

Keep in mind that raw eggs, meats, or any other uncooked foods, are still raw once they are rehydrated, so they either need to be cooked immediately or refrigerated and treated like any other raw food. Bacteria will begin to grow again. Never eat raw freeze dried meat or eggs.

 Rehydrated raw meat and eggs are still raw. Prep and handle as raw. Do not eat raw freeze-dried meat or eggs without first cooking to proper temperatures.

FOODS THAT ARE FREEZE DRIED ARE IN A FORM OF STASIS UNTIL WATER IS ADDED BACK TO THE FOOD.

Chapter 2
Ideas To Get You Started

The Possibilities Are Endless

Here are a few ideas to get you started!

Get your creative juices flowing, and before you know it, you will be creating your own amazing freeze-dried snacks, treats and meals or whatever else your imagination cooks up!

In this chapter you will find ideas and inspiration for:

SNACKS
BREAKFAST
LUNCH
DINNER
DESSERTS
SMOOTHIES
HERBS

Snacks
CANDIES AND TREATS

Milk Duds®

Skittles®

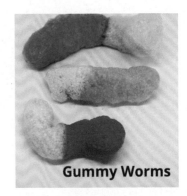
Gummy Worms

Saltwater Taffy

Ice Cream Sandwich

Ice Cream

CHEESE

Don't limit your cheese to just cheddar. For best results, shred cheese or crumble it into small pieces.

Either shredded, or as small pieces prepared as crunchy snacks, cheese packs a high protein punch.

Try These Delicious Cheese Combos:

BLUE CHEESE & FETA
BLUE CHEESE & PEPPER JACK
FLAVORED OR HERBED GOAT CHEESE
MUENSTER & FONTINA
GOUDA & MEDIUM CHEDDAR
SHARP CHEDDAR & SWISS
GRUYÈRE & PROVOLONE
RICOTTA & RACLETTE

OATMEAL APPLE BITES

A nutritious snack for any time of day. For the recipe, see page 100!

COTTAGE CHEESE + FRUIT

Did you know that cottage cheese freeze dries beautifully? Now you can take it anywhere, without needing to refrigerate it.

For a protein-packed healthy snack, combine rehydrated freeze dried cottage cheese with the fruits of your choice.

14

VEGGIE CHIPS

All veggies can easily be made into a healthy snack with a little spritz of olive oil and a dash of seasonings like salt, lemon pepper, pre-packaged seasonings, or even cinnamon. Just slice and spritz with olive oil and sprinkle with your favorite seasoning or spice, then freeze dry.

FRUIT MEDLEY ON-THE-GO

Whatever your favorite fruits are, freeze dry and combine them for a healthy boost of vitamins and flavor anytime, anywhere. You can freeze dry fruits and berries and mix them in any combination!

Breakfast

Here are some delicious breakfast favorites that are easy to freeze dry and keep on hand for use anywhere you happen to be!

Shown clockwise from top:

- Warm up a bowl of oatmeal and sprinkle with freeze-dried fruit.

- Sausages split in half and freeze dried can be rehydrated and grilled, or cut and added to a breakfast scramble or bake.

- French toast: Use freeze-dried powdered eggs and add rehydrated freeze-dried milk, then combine and cook using fresh or freeze-dried bread.

- Eggs can be scrambled, cooked and seasoned before freeze drying; rehydrate them for a quick breakfast.

OATMEAL WITH FRUIT

SAUSAGE LINKS

SCRAMBLED EGGS

FRENCH TOAST

BEEF STEW

SLICED HAM

FRENCH BREAD

Lunch

Portable, easy to rehydrate, and ready for anything. With a Harvest Right home freeze dryer, you've always got lunch covered!

Shown counterclockwise from top

• Beef stew is perfect for an outdoor lunch after a long day of hiking.

• Freeze-dried ham slices and freeze-dried bread can be rehydrated for sandwiches.

• Bakes and casseroles can be freeze dried. Just rehydrate and quickly warm them up in the oven or microwave.

• Freeze-dried avocados make incredible guacamole. Just rehydrate, add fresh or freeze dried ingredients to taste, and serve with chips.

RICE CASSEROLE

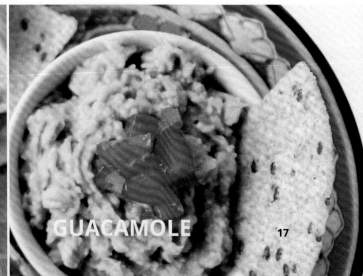

GUACAMOLE

Dinner

Need inspiration for amazing, easy dinners? You can freeze dry meals fully assembled and pre-cooked, or as individual ingredients, ready to prep, combine, and serve!

Shown clockwise from top, left page:

- Mac & cheese casserole - just add water and heat!

- Easy, cheesy scalloped potato bake - just add water and heat!

- Ham dinner with sides of peas and mashed potatoes, shown rehydrated.

- Salmon with pesto, pre-cooked and shown ready to rehydrate.

- Rehydrated sloppy joe meat served with a side of coleslaw and rehydrated mac & cheese.

- Rehydrated turkey dinner with turkey slices, stuffing, potatoes, gravy, green beans, and corn.

MAC & CHEESE

TURKEY DINNER

SLOPPY JOE MEAL

CHEESY POTATOES

PESTO SALMON

HAM DINNER

19

Wow Your Guests With

A Freeze-Dried Meal

HERE'S WHAT WAS FREEZE DRIED IN THIS MEAL:

- ROASTED TURKEY BREAST
- GRAVY
- ASPARAGUS AND CHEESE SAUCE
- WILD RICE
- KALE
- MAC & CHEESE
- LEMON SLICES (FOR LEMONADE)
- PEAS, CORN, AND TOMATO MEDLEY

FLAVORED FROSTING

STRAWBERRY CAKE

22

ECLAIRS WITH FLAVORED FILLING

CHOCOLATE-DIPPED ICE CREAM & STRAWBERRIES

Desserts

Whether your dessert incorporates freeze-dried items or features them as the main attraction, here are some creative, fun ideas that are sure to surprise and intrigue!

Shown counterclockwise from top:

• Cakes, muffins, and frosting flavored with powdered freeze-dried fruit.

• Frosted strawberry cake with flavored frosting decorated with freeze-dried strawberry slices.

• Freeze-dried fruit chopped up and added to eclair filling, topped with melted chocolate.

• Freeze-dried ice cream and freeze-dried fruit dipped in fresh melted chocolate.

• Delicious (and crunchy) freeze-dried cheesecake bites.

FREEZE DRIED CHEESECAKE BITES

Smoothies

Freeze dry your favorite smoothies or just the ingredients. Freeze-dried ingredients can easily be ground into a powder and stored. When ready to use, add to your favorite smoothie base, mix, and serve.

You can also make smoothie bites by pouring smoothie mix into silicone molds and freeze drying. These make a delicious, crunchy snack (see page 109).

Herbs

Instead of using store-bought dried herbs in your recipes, use herbs you've freeze dried. Crushed or flaked, use as a garnish or in the recipe itself. Adding freeze-dried herbs is a delicious, preservative-free way to infuse your dishes with flavor. Freeze-dried herbs are just as flavorful as fresh.

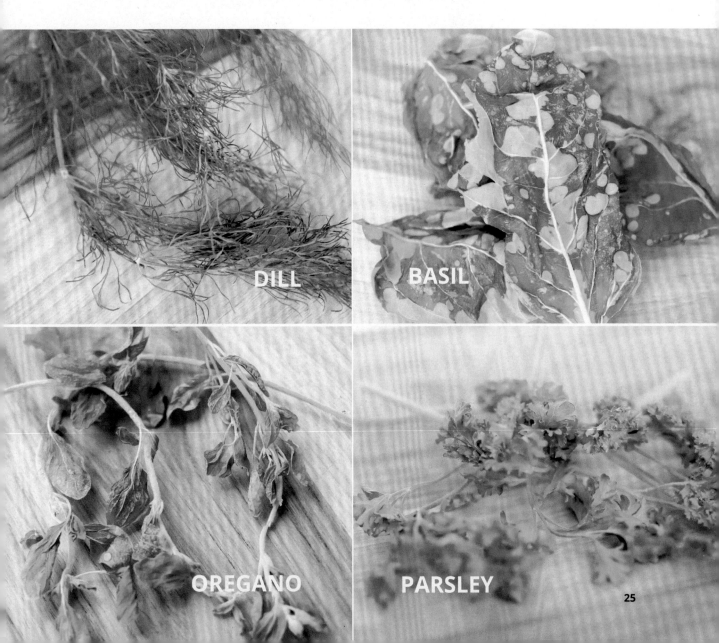

DILL

BASIL

OREGANO

PARSLEY

Chapter 3
Your Lifestyle

Outdoors

Freeze-Dried Meals Can Travel Everywhere!

There is no reason why you can't enjoy your favorite meals at your next campsite: you can freeze dry lightweight, easy-to-prepare meals that will taste fantastic. You can eat as well in the wild as you do at home.

Plus, avid hunters and fishermen know they can end up with too much meat or fish all at once. Now you can freeze dry any extra, whether cooked or raw. When you rehydrate the food, you won't know the difference between fresh and freeze dried.

Favorite Camping Meals and Snacks To Freeze Dry:

- Fresh Fruit Cut Into Bite-Size Pieces

- Mac & Cheese

- Chili

- Scrambled Eggs with Chopped Vegetables and Cheese

- Soup

- Chicken and Rice Casserole

- Scalloped Potatoes and Ham

- Loaded Baked Potato Soup

- Lasagna

- Baked Salmon, Mashed Potatoes, and Asparagus

- Trail Mix With Nuts, Coconut Flakes, and Freeze-Dried Fruits

- Freeze-Dried Fruit Mix

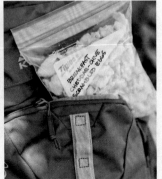

Babies & Toddlers

Make and Freeze Dry Healthy Food
For Your Little Ones

Ensure you always have healthy, fresh-tasting,
preservative-free food on hand anytime, anywhere!

Simple Baby Food Ideas

Blend 1 cup of cooked or steamed peas with 1 cup water. Freeze dry.

Blend 2 cups cooked carrots or squash with 1 cup water. Freeze dry.

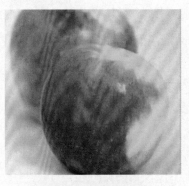

Blend 1 baked apple with 1 cup water. Freeze dry.

TO FREEZE DRY: Combine and blend each group of ingredients and spread the mixture evenly on a freeze dryer tray. Once rehydrated, powder in a blender or break into pieces and store in Mylar bags or Mason jars with an oxygen absorber.

TO REHYDRATE: Mix with water in increments until the desired consistency is achieved.

Freeze-dried applesauce drops are a healthy and portable snack. Just rehydrate when you're ready to eat them!

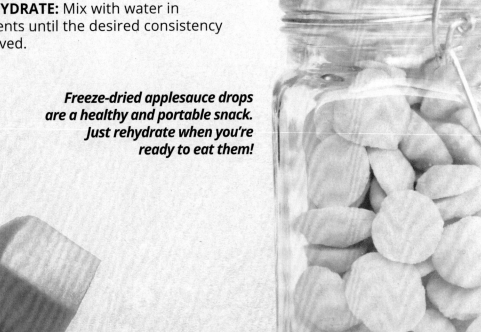

Pet Food

GENERAL TIPS:

Cut the fat off of meats to make sure they freeze dry well and don't go rancid in storage.

You can obtain scraps of liver and other meat scraps from your local butcher.

Cats and dogs love the flavor of nutritional yeast. Toss some into anything you prepare for them. Try tossing freeze-dried veggie cubes with a little nutritional yeast. Pets find the flavor irresistible.

Dogs

Freeze dry raw or cooked meats, with or without added rice, eggs, or vegetables, for healthy meals and treats.

Food "Pucks": Mix ground meats with small amounts of vegetables or egg. Measure into 2 ounce "pucks" wet, then freeze dry. Serve to your dog at mealtime.

Chicken, Turkey, Liver and Beef Cubes: Dice leftover meat in 1" cubes (or smaller if you have a small dog). Place on trays in a single layer and process. No need to rehydrate – dogs love the crunch.

Low-Calorie Squash Treats: Most dogs love any kind of squash, and it's so low in calories that you can feel good about tossing a squash treat any time he begs. Pumpkin can help settle an upset tummy, and freeze-dried pumpkin is also healthy for older dogs who need help with digestive issues.

Reptiles

A protein diet is required for reptiles:

Crickets and mealworms are easily freeze dried, ensuring you always have food on hand for your reptiles.

Cats

Taurine is a must for cats. It can be found in muscle meat and organs like heart, kidney and liver as well as seafood. Feed your cat cubed meats and you can even mix in a little nutritional yeast.

Fish Treats: For salmon, dice fillets into 1/4" bits. For canned tuna, just spread the contents of the can (water and all) onto the freeze drying trays and process. When it's done, break up the freeze-dried tuna into bite-size pieces.

Birds

"Chop" is a mixture of vegetables, cooked grains, legumes, and dry ingredients pulsed in a food processor.

Grains and legumes (cooked): Oats, rye, barley, quinoa, spelt, chickpeas, beans, and lentils.

Dry Ingredients: Millet, chia seed, oats, barley flakes, sesame seed, flax seed, and nuts.

Raw vegetables: Broccoli, kale, parsley, sprouts, carrots, pumpkin, sweet potato, snap peas, beans, corn, and tomato.

The chop ratio should be about 50% vegetables, 40% cooked grains/legumes and 10% dry ingredients. Freeze dry and then reconstitute with small amounts of water.

Always check with your vet before adding any new foods to your pet's diet.

Special Diets

Take Control By Freeze Drying Food For Your Unique Dietary Needs

Your Harvest Right home freeze dryer helps make sure you always have access to fresh, tasty food that supports your dietary needs and restrictions.

Freeze-dried food is perfect for those who eat gluten-free, raw food, vegan, vegetarian, or paleo diets, or those who suffer from food allergies.

Avoid Food Additives:

Prepackaged, processed meals typically include the following added ingredients that you don't want in your meals:

Sodium Nitrate, Maltodextrin, Monosodium Glutamate, High Fructose Corn Syrup, Hydrolyzed Corn Gluten, Trans Fats, Methylcyclopropene, Astaxanthin, Corn Starch, Food Colorings, Olestra, the list goes on and on.

When you freeze dry at home, your homemade food won't contain any of these unhealthy additives.

Vegetarian Soup Kit

When rehydrated, this vegetarian soup is a warm, delicious addition to a weeknight supper.

INSTRUCTIONS:

Cut vegetables and combine all ingredients, then place on trays and freeze dry. Store all of the ingredients together in a Mason jar to use as a soup starter on your pantry shelf.

Add hot water when ready to use.

This process also works in reverse. You can make the soup first, then freeze dry it for later use.

You can freeze dry any combination of soup or stew ingredients together (like beans, rice, pasta, and veggies), then package them in the same container.

INGREDIENTS:

4 cups	**Combination of zucchini, corn, carrots, and beans**
2 cloves	**Garlic, sauteed**
1 small	**Onion, chopped and sauteed**
1 cup	**Tomatoes**
1 cube	**Vegetable bouillon**
1 cup	**Uncooked rice, orzo, or pasta**
1 tsp	**Oregano**
1 Tbsp	**Basil**

Gifts

Freeze-Dried Foods and Crafts Make Perfect Gifts!

Let your creativity run wild. Here are a few ideas to get you started.

Left to right, clockwise (including facing page): Yogurt drops in decorative jars make a fun and colorful gift. Freeze-dried fresh herbs in decorative labeled jars are great for the cooks in your life. Marshmallows in decorated jars layered with hot chocolate mix are a perfect holiday treat. Also, enjoy freeze-dried farmers market corn or freeze-dried cheesecake bites.

FARMERS
MARKET
Sweet
Corn

AUGUST 2015

Chapter 4
Prep & Package

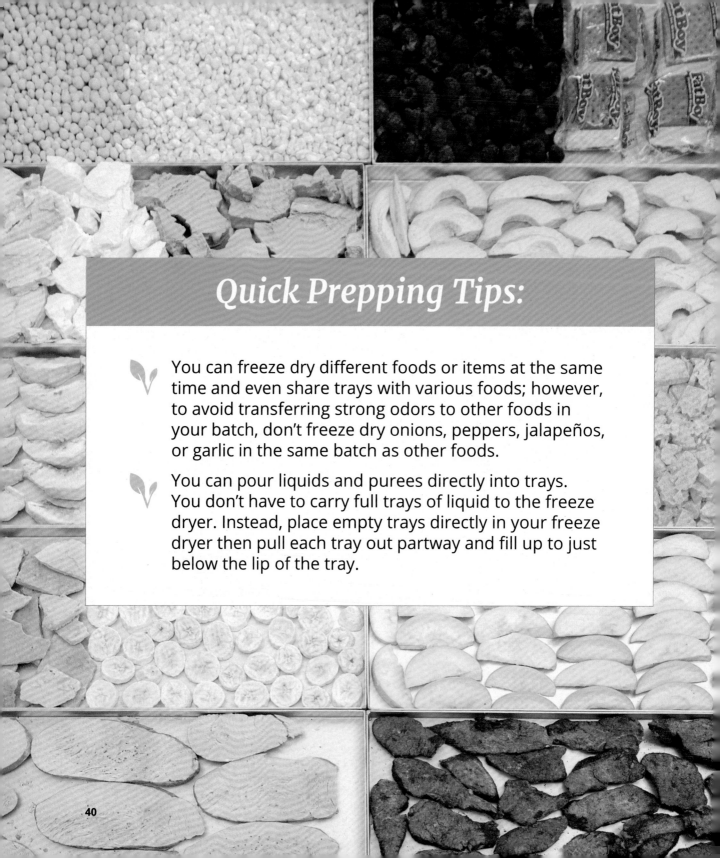

Quick Prepping Tips:

🌱 You can freeze dry different foods or items at the same time and even share trays with various foods; however, to avoid transferring strong odors to other foods in your batch, don't freeze dry onions, peppers, jalapeños, or garlic in the same batch as other foods.

🌱 You can pour liquids and purees directly into trays. You don't have to carry full trays of liquid to the freeze dryer. Instead, place empty trays directly in your freeze dryer then pull each tray out partway and fill up to just below the lip of the tray.

40

Fruits & Berries

Fruit can be freeze dried fresh, frozen, or even canned. Many fruits have a skin, such as grapes and blueberries. These fruits need to be halved, pierced, or sliced to let the moisture out during the freeze drying process. All cut fruits should be placed cut-side up on the trays. If you have canned fruits that are about to expire, you can freeze dry them. They make great treats.

APPLES

Apples can be freeze dried with or without the skin. If you plan to rehydrate the apples for use in cooking, it might be best to remove the skin.

To freeze dry, slice the apples, keeping slices even and under 1/2″ (peeling optional). Place in a bowl of cool water with a bit of lemon to keep them from browning as you work. Once sliced, arrange on your trays. They do not stick to the trays, but they stick to each other, just slightly. They're easy to break apart.

Sprinkling cinnamon or cinnamon sugar on them tastes amazing. You can also powder other fruits like berries or bananas and sprinkle the powder on the apple slices for fun, interesting treats.

Rehydration for cooking:
Place enough cool water in to cover and let sit for 5 minutes, giving them an occasional stir. Once done, use as called for in your recipe.

Applesauce:
Store-bought or homemade applesauce does very well in the freeze dryer. Don't overfill the trays, ensuring you do not exceed the weight limit for your machine. The sauce can stick a little, so you might want to use parchment paper or silicone mats. The final product varies, depending on the amount of sugar in the sauce. Low-sugar applesauces powder better. Higher-sugar content may come out sort of "bendy." Either is fine. For great snacks, you can put applesauce in silicone molds and freeze dry in different shapes.

To rehydrate applesauce, for approximately every 1 ounce of applesauce, use 2 ounces of cool water to start. Stir and if it's the consistency you like, you're done. If not, slowly keep adding water until it is.

Frozen fruits and rehydrated freeze dried food have the same texture. If it can freeze, it can freeze dry.

APRICOTS
Cut in half or into wedges and remove the pit, then place on trays, round side facing down if halved. You can also puree them before freeze drying and use the powder to make syrups or jams.

AVOCADOS
Slice, dice, or mash and place on trays. Avocados can be freeze dried on their own, with or without seasoning them first. Make avocado powder with a blender or food processor after freeze drying, then you can have instant guacamole by simply adding water to the freeze dried powder.

BANANAS
Simply slice them about 3/8" thick, place slices on trays close together, and freeze dry.

BERRIES WITH SKINS
Berries with skins, like blueberries and grapes, require the flesh to be pierced or mashed before freeze drying to prevent them from bursting. If desired, you may choose to blanch for 30 seconds before processing in order to remove the wax from the skin. Before placing in your freeze dryer, blueberries can either be individually pricked with a toothpick (if you want to preserve the shape of the berry), or they can be lightly pulsed in a food processor, slap chopped, or pierced using a berry roller for convenience in processing large batches.

BERRIES WITHOUT SKIN
Berries without skin are easy to process. Simply slice larger berries like strawberries in half, leaving smaller ones like raspberries and blackberries intact. Place them in a single layer on trays and freeze dry.

CHERRIES
Pit and sliced cherries before placing them in one layer on trays.

> **Fruits and berries can be stored whole, crushed, or ground into powder for use as flavorings or add-ins to foods like smoothies and baked goods.**

CITRUS

Use your choice of citrus like oranges, lemons or limes. Cut into thin slices, remove seeds if desired, and place on trays (it's okay to overlap pieces to fit more into each batch). Make sure all the pieces are dry before storing in Mylar bags with an oxygen absorber.

CRANBERRIES

Place 4 cups of fresh whole cranberries and 3 cups of water in a blender and blend for 3 seconds. Drain the cranberries through a sieve and return the water to the blender each time, reusing the same water for 6 pounds of cranberries and adding another cup of fresh water to maintain 3 cups of liquid in the blender. After draining the liquid, place the cranberries onto parchment paper-lined trays. Use a fork to press the cranberry mash down, ensuring that all cranberries are broken open (whole cranberries won't freeze dry well).

FIGS

Cut in half and place on trays, leaving space between each piece.

GRAPES

The skin of the grape needs to be pierced or mashed before freeze drying to prevent bursting in your freeze dryer. Many find that blanching the grapes for a minute or two prior to prepping and freeze drying leads to a better outcome.

It's best to cut grapes in half before freeze drying. Place cut side up on trays. After freeze drying, if the grapes are soft and not hard and crunchy, you'll need to add more time to the dry cycle. Even when they're freeze dried, grapes can seem a little chewy. That's because they have so much sugar.

KIWI

Cut into thin slices and spread out on trays.

MANGO

Cut into slices without the skin. The slices can take a long time to dry, so be sure to leave in the machine until they're dried all the way through and not chewy.

MELONS

Cut watermelon, cantaloupe, and other melons into pieces 1/2" to 3/4" thick and place close together on trays.

OLIVES
Freeze-dried olives can add a nice crunch to salads. Olives don't need to be cut in half if they have been pitted. Rinse first to get rid of excess salt and place on trays to process. Note that the flavor will be much stronger after freeze drying.

PAPAYA
Peel and cut into smaller pieces, then spread out across the trays. Seasonings can be added beforehand.

PEACHES, NECTARINES, ETC
Peel, pit, and slice, placing fruit slices on their sides across the trays.

PEARS
You can leave the skin on and slice similarly to apples. You may choose to soak slices in lemon juice and water to prevent browning.

PINEAPPLE
Pre-freeze pineapple for a quicker dry time. Fresh pineapple freeze dries better than canned, but if you're using canned, be sure to completely drain the juice before processing. Once freeze dried, check to be sure all pieces are completely dry. If any of the pineapple is wet, more dry time is needed. Be certain all pieces are completely dry before storing in jars or Mylar bags.

PLUMS
Remove pits and cut into slices. If worried about tartness, sprinkle with sugar before processing.

POMEGRANATE
Make sure to line your trays to prevent sticking. When freeze drying pomegranate juice, pre-freeze solid before freeze drying.

PRE-FREEZING:
All foods may be pre-frozen to speed up the freeze drying process. You should pre-freeze for at least 24 hours before placing in freeze dryer.

Vegetables & Beans

Most vegetables require rinsing and optional cooking or blanching (except potatoes, which DO require blanching or cooking). Then chop or slice and place on trays. You can freeze dry fresh, canned, or frozen vegetables.

ASPARAGUS
Blanch or slightly grill, season if desired, then place on trays in a single layer. They can be rehydrated or eaten as a crunchy snack.

BEANS
Cook beans (such as black, navy or pinto) prior to freeze drying or use canned beans. It's a good idea to line your trays with parchment paper or use silicone tray liners. Beans can be powdered to make instant refried beans.

BEETS
Blanch, peel, slice, and freeze dry.

BELL PEPPERS
These can be seeded and diced and freeze dried raw.

BROCCOLI
Blanch or cook first, then place on trays in a single layer and process in freeze dryer.

BRUSSELS SPROUTS
Blanch or cook first, then place on trays in a single layer and process in freeze dryer.

CABBAGE
Cut into small slices, stack, or layer up to lip of tray and freeze dry. Can be eaten dry like chips or rehydrated for use in soups and such.

CARROTS
Blanch or cook first for a more airy texture. Cut into thin slivers or chop into small pieces and space out evenly on trays.

CAULIFLOWER
Freeze dry either raw or cooked. To freeze dry cauliflower "rice," pulse florets into granules, spread on trays, and process.

CELERY
Chop or slice raw celery into small pieces and pile on trays up to the lip of each tray.

EGGPLANT
Cut into thin slices or small pieces, season if desired, and place on trays.

GARLIC
Slice and place on trays. Freeze-dried garlic can be powdered. Do not freeze dry with other foods. If you want to get rid of the smell, wash your freeze dryer with mild soapy water.

GREEN BEANS
Green beans rehydrate better when blanched or cooked before freeze drying.

KALE AND LEAFY GREENS
Blanch first or freeze dry raw. Remove stems from larger greens and stack on trays up to the lip of each tray. Store whole or powdered. May be used as an ingredient in other recipes.

MUSHROOMS
Slice or dice and pile on trays. May be used like croutons in salads. May also be rehydrated in soups, stews, spaghetti sauces and other dishes.

ONIONS
Make sure to take the peel off and dice. Pile on trays. If onions are caramelized, pre-freeze them before placing in freeze dryer.

PEAS
Fresh peas should be quickly blanched. This allows the water to escape much more easily. Frozen peas purchased from the store have already been blanched and can be immediately freeze dried. Peas and corn can be piled on trays up to the lip of each tray.

PEPPERS, HOT
All peppers can be freeze dried. When cutting and seeding hot peppers, it is a good idea to wear rubber gloves. Don't freeze dry in the same batch as other foods.

You can freeze dry canned or frozen vegetables purchased from the store. Simply drain, rinse, and place on trays as usual. Stock up when these items are on sale to add to your long-term food storage! Freeze dry before they expire to avoid wasting canned goods.

POTATOES

Blanch or cook potatoes before freeze drying for best results; otherwise, raw potatoes will oxidize and turn black when rehydrated. Slice or dice whole potatoes, or cook them and mash, then spread out on trays. Grated, cooked freeze-dried potatoes make great hashbrowns when rehydrated and browned.

RADISHES

Cut into slices before placing on trays.

SPINACH

Blanch first if you want to keep the leaves from powdering.

SQUASH (SUMMER AND WINTER)

Blanch summer squash and cook winter squash, then slice or dice and place on trays. The skin on summer squash does not rehydrate well, so unless you're shredding them, we recommend that you peel them first. They do not stick to each other, so they can be layered on the trays.

Cubed:

Peel, then cut into 1/2" squares and place on trays. To rehydrate, cover in boiling water and let sit covered for 5 minutes. Add more time as needed. These can be used in soups, stews, breaded and fried, or simply sauteed in butter.

Sliced:

Peel, then cut into 1/4" slices and place on trays. Can be used to replace noodles in things like lasagna. You can freeze dry them in noodle form, but they are really delicate.

Shredded:

To rehydrate shredded summer squash, place squash in a colander and spray warm water on while gently stirring. They only take a minute or two to rehydrate. Pat dry with a paper towel. These can be used for breads, cakes, stir fry, and our favorite, zucchini fritters.

SWEET POTATOES

Blanch and slice into uniform pieces. You can also slice thinly to make chips, or cook and mash.

TOMATOES

All types of tomatoes have a membrane, so they need to be sliced or diced (or halved if they are cherry tomatoes). Then place them, cut side up, on trays.

TOMATO SAUCE

Blanch and peel tomatoes. Add salt, blend for 15 to 20 seconds, then freeze dry.

Meat, Poultry & Fish

It is very important when freeze drying meats, poultry, or fish to clearly label the meat as raw or cooked. Raw freeze-dried meat is still raw and must be either refrigerated or immediately cooked as soon as it is rehydrated. Cooked meat, poultry, or fish can simply be rehydrated and eaten right away, either cold or warm.

BEEF, CHICKEN, PORK, ETC
Remove as much bone and fat as possible. Cut into manageable pieces. We recommend that meat is not thicker than the sides of the trays (3⁄4"). Cooked meat rehydrates in a couple of minutes in hot water. Raw meat should be submerged in water or broth, covered, and placed in the refrigerator overnight.

BACON
Cook, remove as much grease as possible, and lay the bacon on a couple of layers of paper towels in the trays. Bacon will not have as long a shelf life as other foods due to the high fat content. Freeze-dried bacon bits can be used as toppings on salads and other foods.

SAUSAGE
Cooked or raw sausage may be freeze dried. If cooked, remove as much grease as possible after cooking. Then simply slice in half or in pieces and place on the trays.

FISH
Cooked or raw fish fillets may be freeze dried.

> **!** **IMPORTANT: Clearly label any meats as RAW if they are freeze dried uncooked. Raw meat is still raw when rehydrated. The freeze drying process does NOT kill bacteria.**

Grains

COOKED CORN
Cook and add seasoning if desired. Corn may be piled up to the lip of the tray and freeze dried. It can be enjoyed rehydrated, used in recipes, or eaten dry as a delicious, crunchy snack.

COOKED OATMEAL
Cook plain, or add your favorite ingredients such as spices or fruits, then spread on trays.

COOKED RICE OR QUINOA
Cook plain, season, or include in a recipe if desired. Place on trays piled up to the lip of each tray and freeze dry. Plain rice, quinoa, or other cooked grains should be cooked, then quickly rinsed for 10 seconds before placing on trays to keep the grains from sticking together.

COOKED HOMINY
Season, cook and spread on trays. It's delicious as a crunchy snack or rehydrated.

Herbs

Freeze dry your favorite herbs for use in recipes or as garnishes.

TIPS FOR HERBS:

Herbs are delicate and can be piled on trays (as high as the lip of each tray). They freeze dry rather quickly compared to other foods.

Cut into smaller pieces or use individual leaves and place on trays with a paper towel on top to keep them from blowing off the trays.

Freeze-dried herbs are easy to crush and bottle.

Complete Meals

Casseroles, lasagnas, rice dishes, and nearly any other delicious meal can easily be freeze dried.

CASSEROLES

Casseroles freeze dry well as long as they are not overly greasy. You'll need to watch how thick the casserole is so that it freeze dries all the way through. The thicker the product is, the harder it is to freeze dry, so try and keep things about a half-inch thick for faster dry times. Casseroles with meat tend to take longer to freeze dry.

SOUPS & STEWS

Make or purchase your favorite soups or stews, then pour into trays, filling about halfway, and freeze dry.

To rehydrate, add water to the consistency desired and simmer on the stove.

You Can Freeze Dry Fermented Foods

For many years, kraut and pickles were canned for long-term preservation, but the good bacteria which ferment the kraut (and the corresponding health benefits) were lost when the ferments were heated in canning.

Imagine for a moment, having sauerkraut or curtido that is *exactly* at the point of fermentation that you love. You know that you can't eat it all right away, and even though it will be good for a few months, it will evolve and change over time. Now, you simply freeze dry it and you still have that exact flavor you love. In addition, nearly all the nutritional benefits will still be intact.

Dairy

Freeze drying dairy allows you to create a shelf-stable supply of milk as well as your favorite cheeses and yogurts.

MILK

If not frozen solid, milk will bubble in the freeze dryer and make a mess. You might want to put it in the freezer to pre-freeze before freeze drying.

SOUR CREAM AND YOGURT

For yogurt, sour cream, or other similar products, spread a thick, even layer on a freeze drying tray and freeze dry. The freeze dried product will sift into a fine powder. Yogurt drops can be made using a piping bag and stored as easy-to-eat bites. Yogurt may also be freeze dried into fun shapes using silicone molds. Yogurts with a higher sugar content seem to hold their shape better.

RICOTTA AND COTTAGE CHEESE

Simply spread on trays in a thick layer.

Eggs

Eggs can be freeze dried after cooking for quick eating or raw for powdering and adding to recipes. Raw freeze-dried eggs are still raw when rehydrated and must either be refrigerated or cooked immediately.

For cooked eggs, simply scramble as normal, transfer to trays, and freeze dry. When cooking, you can add cheese, peppers, and other seasonings prior to freeze drying.

For raw eggs, beat them and pour directly into the trays. When the freeze dry cycle is over, you can blend the eggs into powder, but it isn't necessary. They store just fine without being powdered.

Packaging Tips:

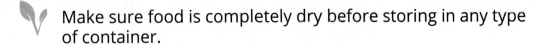

- Make sure food is completely dry before storing in any type of container.

- Store food immediately after freeze drying.

- Break a larger piece in half to ensure complete dryness. Once confirmed dry, do not let food sit out for very long, or it will begin to rehydrate from natural moisture in the air.

- Once a container has been opened, the oxygen absorber no longer works and should be replaced before resealing the container for long-term storage.

- It's easier to write on Mylar bags before filling with food.

- You shouldn't use an oxygen absorber and a desiccant in the same jar or bag.

- A full-size Mylar bag that is cut into quarters makes the perfect snack bag. Be sure all sides have an adequate seal.

MYLAR BAGS

USE: LONG-TERM STORAGE

For longest storage life, Mylar bags are a great solution. Place food into Mylar bags, add the appropriate oxygen absorber, and seal. Mylar bags can be opened and resealed.

#10 CANS

USE: LONG-TERM STORAGE

These require an investment in a can sealer but can be a really great option for long-term bulk food storage.

CANNING JARS

USE: MEDIUM- AND LONG-TERM STORAGE

Perfect for medium- and long-term storage when stored with an oxygen absorber, out of the light in a dark, cool location like a pantry or basement.

RESEALABLE JARS

USE: SHORT-TERM STORAGE

Many freeze-dried foods are perfect as a snack when stored in airtight containers, even without oxygen absorbers.

Tips For Trays

🌱 When freeze drying liquids such as milk, raw scrambled eggs, or soups, it works better to place empty trays into the freeze dryer first, then pull out slightly and fill up with liquids or place in freezer, pour in liquids, and pre-freeze.

🌱 Having extra sets of trays can help you save leftovers in the freezer so you'll always be ready with your next batch to freeze dry.

🌱 Make sure all trays have food. Freeze drying with empty trays will cause the freeze dryer to think food is completely dry before the trays with food are dry.

🌱 When pre-freezing, you can stack trays in the freezer using plastic wrap to cover the trays. You may also purchase plastic tray lids.

Weighing In: Use a Kitchen Scale to Calculate Rehydration

Using a kitchen scale to weigh food before and after freeze drying allows you to calculate how much water to add back in when rehydrating.

 Measure weights in ounces for easy calculation.

 Remember to account for the weight of the trays or containers you are weighing your food in. Weigh your food in the same container before and after processing.

1. Before loading trays with food, measure the weight of the tray or container your fresh food is in (when empty) and make note of it for future reference.

2. Measure the weight of the fresh food you are placing on each tray and make note of that. You can weigh the food in the container or tray you've already weighed. Then simply subtract the weight of the container or tray which gives you the food weight.

3. Process the food in your freeze dryer.

4. Repeat the weighing process with the freeze-dried food, again taking into account the weight of the tray or container. The weight of the freeze-dried food (minus the weight of the tray or container) represents the weight of the water that the freeze drying process eliminated.

5. Subtract the weight of the dried food from the weight of the fresh food. This gives you the weight of the water that you'll be eventually adding back during rehydrating.

6. Once you have the weight of the water, divide that number by the weight in ounces of the dried food. This gives you the amount of water you'll need to rehydrate each ounce of dried food.

Sample Calculation, Per Ounce

Weight of Empty Tray: **26.2 oz.**
Weight of Filled Tray, Fresh: **47.4 oz.**
Weight of Filled Tray, Dry: **30.4 oz.**

Weight of **Fresh** Food minus Tray: **21.2 oz**
Weight of **Dried** Food minus Tray: **4.2 oz**

Fresh minus **Dried** tells you how much water was removed during freeze drying:

21.2 oz. Fresh – 4.2 oz. Dried
=
17 oz. Water Removed

Divide the weight of the **Dried** by the weight of the **Water Removed** to calculate how many ounces of water are needed to rehydrate each ounce.

17 oz. Water Removed ÷ 4.2 oz. Dried
=
approx. 4 oz. Water
to Rehydrate 1 oz. Dried

Chapter 5
How To Rehydrate

Basics of Rehydrating

SOUP, CHILI, STEW, AND SPAGHETTI SAUCE

Rehydrating these items is easy. Just add the amount of hot water that brings the soup, stew, or spaghetti sauce to the consistency you prefer. You can save a little of the freeze-dried food off to the side so that if you added too much water, you can add some more of the dry ingredients.

When adding freeze-dried ingredients to a recipe that already has water/liquid, like soup or spaghetti sauce, just add in the freeze-dried ingredients and add 2 to 4 tablespoons of extra water for every cup of freeze-dried food. The freeze-dried food will rehydrate while the food simmers.

MEAT, POULTRY, FISH

If you are rehydrating freeze-dried meat, poultry, or fish that has already been *cooked*, place it in a bowl and add enough hot water to completely cover the food. If the pieces/slices are thin, they will rehydrate in 3 to 4 minutes. If the pieces are thick, it may take 6 to 10 minutes. You can test it with a fork to see if it feels rehydrated.

Raw meats and fish should be placed in a container or bowl and submerged in cold water or broth, then covered and placed in the refrigerator overnight. Once it is rehydrated, you can take it out of the water and pat it off with a paper towel. It is then ready to be cooked. Because it is raw, it should be used right away.

MASHED POTATOES, STUFFING AND RICE

These are easy to rehydrate. Place the food in a bowl and add hot water to the desired consistency. Cover and let stand for 3 to 4 minutes. Fluff with a fork.

MAC & CHEESE AND OTHER PASTA DISHES

Some of the more difficult things to rehydrate are dishes with pasta in them. It is best to place these items in a casserole dish, add hot water, stir, cover with foil, and bake for 30 to 35 minutes in a preheated oven at 350°F. This same process works well for thick casseroles, scalloped potatoes, and stews. Lasagna can't be stirred in water unless you don't mind messing it up. To rehydrate it so that it still looks nice, you can pour water in the bottom of the casserole dish and it will steam the lasagna while it bakes.

POWDERED ITEMS SUCH AS AVOCADO, RAW EGGS, SMOOTHIES, SOUR CREAM, AND YOGURT

To rehydrate these items, just place them in a bowl and add cool water to reach the desired consistency. Raw egg powder is easy to rehydrate. For the equivalent of one egg, add 2 tablespoons of freeze-dried egg powder to 2 tablespoons of cool water and stir.

REHYDRATING ON THE GO

Many foods can be rehydrated by pouring boiling water directly into the Mylar bag. This works great for camping or backpacking.

Rehydrating Tips

- Keep a spray bottle on hand that you can fill with clean water to use for rehydrating. It's perfect for gently spritzing delicate leafy greens and herbs back to life.

- Vegetables may be microwaved in water to speed up rehydration. This works for other foods, too.

- Foods like breads and cakes can be freeze dried then gently rehydrated by wrapping them in a moist paper towel that is then sealed in a plastic bag and stored in the fridge.

- Raw or cooked meats rehydrate to the same level of freshness they were before freeze drying. Rehydrate meats by submerging/soaking in water or broth. Rehydrated raw meat is still raw, so once it is rehydrated, prep, store, and handle as raw. Rehydrate in the fridge.

- The best way to hydrate most freeze-dried foods is to add just enough hot or cold water for it to begin to "pool" at the bottom. Then, stir occasionally. For most foods, this will be enough to reconstitute it as close to fresh as possible.

Fruits & Berries

Raw fruit can be freeze dried fresh or frozen.

Freeze-dried fruit can be added directly to things like smoothies, cold cereal (with milk), or hot oatmeal. It will naturally rehydrate.

Or, rehydrate fruit by placing it in a bowl filled with cool water, cover, and let sit until rehydrated. In addition, you can add water a little at a time and stir to proper consistency. Rehydrated fruit can be used in recipes like pies and cobblers.

Vegetables

You can freeze dry vegetables whether they are raw or cooked.

To rehydrate raw vegetables, place them in a large bowl filled with cool water. Cover and let sit. Foods like green beans may take a few hours. Once the vegetables are rehydrated, you can prepare them as you would fresh vegetables.

Cooked vegetables are easy to rehydrate. Place them in hot water for a few minutes, drain, and eat. You can throw the dry, raw, or cooked vegetables into soups, stews, chili, or spaghetti sauces.

Eggs

Eggs can be freeze dried raw or cooked. Powdered raw eggs can be used in recipes and both powdered and/or broken-up freeze-dried eggs can be used for scrambling.

To rehydrate *raw egg* powder, approximately 2 tablespoons of egg powder plus 2 tablespoons of water equals one egg. Simply mix egg and water and add to any recipe, or scramble as usual.

For *pre-cooked eggs*, place broken-up freeze-dried eggs in a frying pan and slowly add water or warm milk to rehydrate. Once rehydrated, cook eggs until warm or just place in a bowl, add hot water, and stir.

Bread

Carefully rehydrating bread will bring it back to its original texture.

Wrap bread with a damp paper towel, put it inside a plastic bag in the fridge, and it will rehydrate overnight.

Or, wrap the bread in a damp kitchen towel, and let it sit on your counter, checking periodically to see when it's fully rehydrated.

If you're making stuffing, just add your spices and then slowly add hot water and stir until it reaches the proper consistency.

For French toast, let the bread soak in an egg and milk mixture until it softens, then fry in a frying pan like usual.

Meat & Seafood

You have the option to cook meats before freeze drying, or leave them raw. Just remember that freeze drying doesn't remove bacteria. Be sure to clearly label meat that was freeze dried in a raw state.

 IMPORTANT: Raw rehydrated meat is still raw, so prep and handle accordingly. Do not eat raw, uncooked freeze-dried meat.

COOKED MEAT
Place cooked freeze-dried meat inside a bowl filled with hot or warm water or broth. Let the meat absorb water until tender (takes just a few minutes). It may be eaten right away or used in cooking.

RAW MEAT
If meat was freeze dried raw, after rehydrating it you should refrigerate it, or prepare and eat it as you would any fresh meat. Place raw meat in a bowl of cold water and place in the fridge overnight or until rehydrated.

SAUSAGES AND PEPPERONI
Place freeze-dried cooked sausage or pepperoni inside a bowl filled with hot water. Let the meat absorb water until tender (takes just a few minutes). It may be eaten right away or used in cooking.

SANDWICH MEAT
Place in a bowl of warm water. It will rehydrate in 2 or 3 minutes. Pat off with a paper towel.

 COOKED MEAT should be rehydrated in warm or hot water.

 RAW MEAT should be rehydrated in cold water in the fridge.

Dairy

There are many uses for freeze-dried dairy ingredients.

MILK
Powder to avoid lumps. Add cold water to taste in freeze-dried milk powder, or measure your milk before placing in the freeze dryer and note the amounts on your packaging. For example, 2 cups of liquid milk that is freeze dried will equal 2 cups of rehydrated milk (this ratio includes the freeze-dried milk powder plus water).

YOGURT AND SOUR CREAM
Add water to finely powdered freeze-dried yogurt or sour cream and it will return to its original, fresh state. Add water gradually and stir until it is the desired consistency.

COTTAGE CHEESE
Rehydrate by adding cold milk or water. Refrigerate while rehydrating.

HARD CHEESES
Fold grated cheese directly into baked goods, pastas or casseroles. Or, wrap sliced cheese in a moist paper towel to rehydrate to its original state.

Freeze-dried sour cream

Freeze-dried shredded cheese

Soups & Stews

An easy meal for any occasion!

Gradually add hot water or broth to your freeze-dried soup or stew until it reaches desired consistency. Soups can be premade and then freeze dried, or individual freeze-dried ingredients can be packaged as a kit.

Casseroles & Pastas

Make casseroles or pasta ahead of time and freeze dry for use later as a simple meal.

Preserve a casserole or pasta dish, like creamy alfredo pasta, and rehydrate at a moment's notice. You can apply this with any similar dish like lasagna, ravioli, or spaghetti and meatballs.

When you're ready to eat your casserole or pasta, transfer to any casserole dish and add about 1 cup of warm water per tray.

Cover with foil and bake in the oven at 350°F for 30-35 minutes, stirring periodically. Continue checking until proper consistency is achieved.

For small servings, add hot water, warm in the microwave, cover, and let sit until pasta has properly rehydrated.

Rice and Rice Dishes

Rice dishes or plain cooked rice can easily be rehydrated for a quick meal.

Rehydrate rice dishes by slowly adding hot water or hot broth to reach desired consistency. Many find that approximately a 1:1 ratio of rice to liquid is about right, but each dish might require experimentation when figuring out how much liquid to add.

You can rehydrate plain rice for use in any recipe that calls for cooked rice.

Leafy Greens & Herbs

Not only can leafy greens like spinach, kale, and herbs be freeze dried, they can also be rehydrated and used fresh, even in salads!

Spritz leafy veggies and herbs back to life in a plastic bag with a spray bottle, then toss and enjoy as you would if fresh, cooked or steamed. The nutrients and taste stay intact. Put leafy veggies directly into a smoothie or blend them into a powder to add to a sauce or soup.

What's For Dinner?

This delicious rehydrated meal was once completely freeze dried!

Ravioli, Tomato Soup, Salad, and Berry Dessert.

69

Chapter 6
Our Favorite Recipes

From Our Kitchen To Yours!

Mom's Chicken Noodle Soup

INSTRUCTIONS:

Bring chicken broth to a boil in a large two-gallon pot. Add cooked egg noodles, chicken, carrots, celery, onion, and seasoning. Simmer on low for 30 minutes. In a separate bowl, whisk together cream of chicken soup and heavy cream. Cool soup a little and add whisked ingredients and butter. Stir until soup is creamy. Enjoy!

If using dry noodles, reduce boiling time to approximately 10 minutes.

INGREDIENTS

4 to 6	**Chicken breasts, cooked and chopped or shredded**
2 cartons	**Chicken broth (32 oz. each)**
24 oz. pkg.	**Frozen egg noodles (thawed) and boiled approx. 20 minutes or dry noodles boiled approx. 10 minutes**
3 cups	**Chopped carrots**
3 cups	**Chopped celery**
1 cup	**Chopped onion**
2 pkgs.	**Dry Italian dressing seasoning**
1 can (10.5 oz.)	**Cream of chicken soup**
½ cube (4 Tbsp)	**Butter**
2 cups	**Heavy cream**
To taste	**Salt and pepper**

Hamburger Chowder

Makes 6-8 servings.

INSTRUCTIONS:

Brown and drain meat.

Combine water, meat, tomatoes, macaroni, Worcestershire sauce, onion, and salt.

Cover and simmer 10 minutes, stirring occasionally.

Add vegetables and simmer 5 to 10 minutes longer, or until beans and macaroni are tender.

Serve sprinkled with cheese.

INGREDIENTS

1 lb.	**Ground beef**
1 qt.	**Water**
1 can (16 oz.)	**Tomatoes**
1 cup	**Elbow macaroni**
2 Tbsp.	**Worcestershire sauce**
1 Tbsp.	**Instant dried onion**
1 tsp.	**Salt**
1 cup	**Frozen vegetables**
	Shredded cheese

Crock-pot Hamburger Soup

INSTRUCTIONS:

Brown hamburger, drain, and rinse.

Dice potatoes and carrots.

Combine soups in a big bowl and mix well.

Combine all ingredients in a large crock-pot (vegetables on the bottom) and cook on low for 10 to 12 hours.

INGREDIENTS

1 lb.	**Hamburger**
5	**Medium potatoes**
6 to 8	**Medium carrots**
1 pkg.	**Dry onion soup mix**
2 cans	**Cream of mushroom soup**
1 can	**Tomato soup**
1 can	**Cream of celery soup**

Hearty Beef and Vegetable Soup

Makes about 12 servings.

INSTRUCTIONS:

Brown meat and onions.

Mix all ingredients and simmer until thoroughly cooked.

INGREDIENTS

1½ lb.	**Lean ground beef**
3	**Onions, chopped**
2	**Ribs celery, diced**
1 qt.	**Water**
2	**Medium carrots, diced**
5	**Potatoes, diced**
1 Tbsp.	**Salt**
½ tsp.	**Pepper**
1 Tbsp.	**Parsley**
1 can (16 oz.)	**Tomatoes**
1 can	**Whole corn**
1 can	**Kidney beans (drained & rinsed)**
1 can (6 oz.)	**Tomato paste**
½ tsp.	**Garlic salt**

Bone Broth

Makes about 2 quarts of broth.

INSTRUCTIONS:

Bring bones and about 6 quarts of water to a boil, then reduce heat to medium and simmer about 1 hour. Skim off surface fat. Add vegetables and herbs and simmer for 2 hours, skimming the surface. Strain the broth through a fine strainer or cheesecloth and let cool. Store for up to a week.

TO FREEZE DRY: Pour the strained liquid onto freeze dryer trays and process. Use a food processor to grind the freeze-dried broth into a powder.

TO REHYDRATE: Add the powder to hot water. Experiment with the ratios according to how strong you like your broth.

INGREDIENTS

6 lbs.	**Chicken, turkey, lamb or beef bones**
2	**Onions, quartered**
4	**Carrots, diced large**
4	**Stalks celery, diced large**
1 large handful	**Parsley**
To taste	**Fresh thyme**
12 oz.	**Tomatoes, quartered**
1 head	**Garlic**
2 tsp.	**Black peppercorns**
2	**Bay leaves**

Cold Watermelon & Ginger Soup

INSTRUCTIONS:

Freeze the diced watermelon for about an hour.

Combine sugar, water, and ginger in a saucepan and simmer for 2 minutes. Purée the frozen watermelon in a blender, then slowly pour in the hot sugar syrup.

Add mint and combine until the soup is liquid. Top with diced honeydew melon.

INGREDIENTS

8 cups	**Diced watermelon in 1½" pieces (about 1 lb.)**
1¾ cups	**Granulated sugar**
¾ cups	**Water**
1 Tbsp.	**Freshly grated ginger, divided**
8 leaves	**Fresh mint**
3 cups	**Crushed ice**
¾ cups	**Honeydew melon, finely diced and chilled**

Tuscan White Bean Soup

INSTRUCTIONS:

The basic ingredients are cannellini beans, diced celery, broth, sautéed onion and garlic, a sprig of rosemary, and a bay leaf. You can add kale if you like. This soup pairs well with a little slice of cornbread for sweetness. To convert this to a summer dish, cook a small pasta in broth with the rosemary and bay leaf, then remove the bay leaf and rosemary. Toss in the other ingredients, including a bit of fresh corn roasted on the grill then cut off the cob.

Freeze dry this in small batches, then add a small drizzle of olive oil right before eating. Enjoy!

Dairy-Free Corn Chowder

A vegan version of classic corn chowder.

INSTRUCTIONS:

Put the potatoes in a pot of boiling water and let them boil until soft. In a stock pot, sauté the onion and garlic in olive oil until translucent.

Reduce to medium heat and add vegetable or chicken stock, corn, carrots, celery, bell pepper, salt, pepper, and oregano.

While the vegetables simmer, drain cooked potatoes and transfer to a blender or food processor and blend until smooth.

Begin to add potato purée to the soup until it's thickened. If you want a traditionally creamier soup, leave the potatoes in a 1" dice and add to soup with the vegetables.

INGREDIENTS

1 bag	**Frozen corn**
2 large	**Potatoes, diced**
3 Tbsp.	**Olive oil**
1 large	**Sweet onion**
4 cloves	**Garlic**
3	**Carrots, peeled and chopped**
3 stalks	**Celery, chopped**
1	**Red bell pepper, cored and diced**
2 tsp.	**Salt**
1 tsp.	**Fresh ground pepper**
1 tsp.	**Oregano**
4 cups	**Vegetable broth**

Traditional Corn Chowder

INSTRUCTIONS:

Add prepared vegetables to 2 cups of water and cook gently until tender.

Make white sauce using margarine, flour, and milk. Add white sauce to cooked vegetables; stir. Add corn. Salt and pepper to taste.

Garnish with favorite toppings.

This recipe can be made using freeze-dried ingredients.

INGREDIENTS

2 cups	**Potatoes**
½ cup	**Celery, cut small**
½ cup	**Onion, cut small**
1 cup	**Carrots, cut small**
2 cups	**Water**
¼ cup	**Margarine**
¼ cup	**Flour**
2 cups	**Milk**
2 cups	**Corn**
To taste	**Salt and pepper**

Curried Butternut Squash Soup Kit

INSTRUCTIONS:

Dice all vegetables. Sauté onion and garlic lightly in olive oil. Combine all ingredients and freeze dry.

TO REHYDRATE: Simmer all ingredients in 6 cups of hot water, then puree in a food processor until smooth. Garnish with salted cashews.

INGREDIENTS

1	**Butternut squash, peeled & diced**
1 small	**Onion**
2 cloves	**Garlic**
2 cubes	**Vegetable bouillon**
1 Tbsp.	**Curry powder**
2	**Ripe bananas, smashed**
¼ cup	**Coconut, shaved**

Hearty Vegetable Soup Kit

INSTRUCTIONS:

Dice all vegetables. Combine all ingredients and freeze dry.

TO REHYDRATE: Add 4-6 cups of water to a stock pot and let simmer. Salt and pepper to taste.

INGREDIENTS

4 cups	**Any combination of freeze-dried zucchini, corn, carrots, beans and potato**
2 cloves	**Garlic, lightly sautéed in olive oil**
1 small	**Onion, lightly sautéed in olive oil with garlic**
1 cup	**Tomatoes**
1 cube	**Vegetable, beef or chicken bouillon**
1 cup	**Rice, orzo or dried pasta**
1 cup	**Dried beans, any kind**
1 tsp.	**Oregano**
1 Tbsp.	**Basil**

Black Bean & Vegetable Chili

Makes 6 servings.

INSTRUCTIONS:

Stir-fry the diced onion and peppers in 1 tablespoon of olive oil for 2 minutes in a stockpot.

Add the green chilies, corn, and garlic, and cook for 1 minute.

Add the rest of the ingredients and simmer for 15 minutes.

Freeze dry in individual portions.

Add a slice of whole grain baguette when you're ready to eat.

INGREDIENTS

4 cups	**Black beans**
1	**Onion, diced**
2 cups	**Vegetable bouillon**
20 oz.	**Tomatoes, diced**
1 cup	**Green chiles**
1 cup	**Corn**
1 cup	**Green and red peppers, diced**
3 cloves	**Garlic**
4 Tbsp.	**Soy sauce**
To taste	**Chili powder, salt, jalapeños**

Jambalaya

You will need to use a large stockpot in order to make this recipe.

INSTRUCTIONS:

Cook vegetables and chicken in the stockpot with a small amount of broth.

After fresh vegetables and chicken are cooked, add the rest of the broth.

Next add diced tomatoes, brown rice, and bay leaves. Add Cajun spice.

Bring to a boil, then cover and simmer for 45 minutes.

Add shrimp and cook for 3 to 4 minutes.

Once cooked, enjoy. Freeze dry the rest.

Once freeze dried, just add boiling water to the portion you want to eat. Because the recipe is a little soupy, you don't have to be precise with the amount of water you add.

INGREDIENTS

9 cups	**Chicken or vegetable broth**
3	**Onions, diced**
12 cloves	**Garlic**
6 stalks	**Celery**
9	**Bell peppers**
6	**Chicken breasts, diced**
3 lbs.	**Shrimp, cut up**
3 cans	**Diced tomatoes**
4½ cups	**Brown rice**
3	**Bay leaves**
6 Tbsp.	**Cajun spice**

Zucchini Casserole

Makes 6-8 servings.

INSTRUCTIONS:

Boil zucchini, carrots, and onions for 5 minutes. Drain.

Cook stuffing; set aside. Mix the cooked vegetables, soup, and sour cream.

Place in 9x13 baking dish. Top with cooked stuffing. Cook at 350°F for 25 minutes.

Note: Chicken, cooked and cubed, may also be added to the vegetable mixture.

INGREDIENTS

6 cups	**Zucchini, cubed**
1 cup	**Carrots, grated**
½ cup	**Onions**
1 can	**Cream of chicken soup**
2 boxes	**Chicken flavored stuffing**
8 oz.	**Sour cream**

Salmon With Summer Pesto

Perfect for an easy Sunday dinner.

INSTRUCTIONS:

PESTO:

Put all ingredients in a food processor and blend until smooth.

SALMON:

Bake or broil salmon fillets for a few minutes until done, add a dollop of pesto sauce and then place the fillets on your freeze dry trays. You may want to line your trays with paper towels to absorb any excess oil from the fillets.

TO FREEZE DRY: Freeze dry as normal, making sure that all of the moisture is removed from the very center of the fish. Store the fillets in an airtight container or in a Mylar bag with an oxygen absorber until you're ready to use them. Make sure to label the container so you know when you freeze dried it. You may want to freeze dry the pesto separate from the salmon so that it doesn't get overly diluted when rehydrating the salmon.

INGREDIENTS

6-8	**Salmon fillets**
¼ cup	**Pine nuts**
9 cloves	**Chopped garlic**
5 cups	**Fresh basil leaves, packed**
1 tsp.	**Kosher salt**
1 tsp.	**Black pepper, freshly ground**
1½ cups	**Olive oil**
1 cup	**Parmesan, freshly grated**

Favorite BBQ Turkey Meatballs

INSTRUCTIONS:

MEATBALLS:

Combine all ingredients, and shape into 2" balls. Broil on a baking sheet for 10 minutes.

SAUCE:

Sauté onion and garlic in coconut oil, then add all other ingredients and simmer until it makes a thick sauce. For improved flavor, make the sauce at least one day ahead to give the flavors time to blend.

You can serve these meatballs in a slow cooker or on sandwiches. They're particularly delicious with spaghetti squash pasta.

INGREDIENTS

Meatballs:

1 lb.	**Ground turkey**
1 slice	**Whole wheat bread, as crumbs**
¼ cup	**Parmesan cheese, grated**
1 clove	**Garlic, minced**
¼ cup	**Onion, minced**
2 tsp	**Fresh thyme**
1	**Egg, beaten**
½ tsp.	**Salt**
½ tsp.	**Black pepper**

Sugar-free BBQ sauce:

1 Tbsp.	**Coconut oil**
1 Tbsp.	**Soy sauce**
1 small	**Onion, diced**
3 cloves	**Garlic, minced**
1 tsp.	**Oregano**
1 tsp.	**Mustard powder**
1 tsp.	**Cumin**
1 tsp.	**Chili powder**
6 oz.	**Tomato paste**
2 cups	**Chicken stock**
2 Tbsp.	**Apple cider vinegar**
1 tsp.	**Truvia or Stevia**

Cauliflower Rice

INSTRUCTIONS:

Place fresh cauliflower florets in a food processor and pulse until the florets break down into granules the size of rice or couscous. Use this "rice" to replace any grain in salads, recipes, or as a base for ethnic dishes. You can also cook cauliflower rice in butter or olive oil to make your favorite version of fried or curried rice. Cauliflower rice is a great way to sneak more vegetables into your diet while hanging on to your favorite rice-based meals.

TO FREEZE DRY: Spread the "rice" on freeze drying trays and process.

TO REHYDRATE: Add warm water until it returns to its original consistency.

Cauliflower Potatoes

INSTRUCTIONS:

Steam or boil cauliflower florets until tender. Drain until almost dry. Add florets to warm milk, garlic, salt, and butter. Blend with a mixer until fluffy.

Cauliflower has a slightly nutty flavor, and because there's no starch, it will never get gummy like over-whipped mashed potatoes. To eliminate dairy, save a cup of the liquid to steam or boil the cauliflower instead of using milk or cream.

TO FREEZE DRY: Spread on freeze drying trays and process.

TO REHYDRATE: Add warm water and stir until it returns to its original consistency.

Grilled Veggies With Dipping Sauces

These five sauce recipes are perfect for giving your grilled veggies flair!

Grill vegetables on a hot grill pan until some edges are charred, then dip, spread, or drizzle these sauces and enjoy!

ITALIAN PARMESAN GRILLING PASTE

INGREDIENTS

½ cup	**Parmesan cheese**
¼ cup	**Olive oil**
¼ cup	**Red wine vinegar**
2 Tbsp.	**Dried basil**
2 Tbsp.	**Dried oregano**
4 cloves	**Garlic, minced**

Combine all ingredients and brush on grilled vegetables.

LEMON-GARLIC AIOLI DIPPING SAUCE

INGREDIENTS

1 cup	**Mayonnaise**
2 Tbsp.	**Lemon zest**
2 Tbsp.	**Lemon juice**
1 tsp.	**White pepper**
2 Tbsp.	**Dried basil**
Sprinkle	**Sea salt**

Combine all ingredients and use as a dipping sauce.

BLUE CHEESE DIPPING SAUCE

INGREDIENTS

2 cups	**Sour cream**
8 oz.	**Blue cheese**
⅔ cup	**Mayonnaise**
3 Tbsp.	**Cider vinegar**
1 tsp.	**Red pepper**
To taste	**Onion salt, celery salt & Worcestershire sauce**

Combine all ingredients and let rest in the fridge overnight. Serve as a dip.

GINGER VINAIGRETTE

INGREDIENTS

3 Tbsp.	**Vegetable stock**
3 Tbsp.	**Lime juice**
3 Tbsp.	**Fresh ginger, grated**
2 Tbsp.	**Shallots, chopped**
1 Tbsp.	**Honey**
1 Tbsp.	**Soy sauce**
1 clove	**Garlic, minced**
2 Tbsp.	**Olive oil**

Combine all ingredients and serve as a dip.

SUN-DRIED TOMATO GOAT CHEESE BUTTER

INGREDIENTS

3 Tbsp.	**Sun-dried tomatoes**
4 oz.	**Goat cheese**

Process in blender or food processor until smooth. Spread on grilled vegetables.

Asparagus With Lemon Verbena Pesto

INSTRUCTIONS:

Put 2 cups of lemon verbena leaves, 1/4 cup of pine nuts, and 1 cup of Parmesan cheese in the food processor or blender. Add olive oil until the mixture makes a paste.

Spread it over rehydrated asparagus.

INGREDIENTS

2 cups	**Fresh lemon verbena leaves**
1 cup	**Grated Parmesan cheese**
¼ cup	**Pine nuts or English walnuts**
	Olive oil
To taste	**Salt**

Lemon Chicken & Grilled Vegetables

Makes 6 servings.

INSTRUCTIONS:

Marinate chicken for 2 hours in lemon juice and zest, olive oil, and rosemary stems.

Grill cutlets, then grill diced vegetables in broiler or on grill pan.

Combine 1 cutlet with 1 cup of grilled vegetables and freeze dry in individual servings.

INGREDIENTS

6	**Chicken breasts**
3	**Lemons, juiced and zested**
4 Tbsp.	**Olive oil**
3 stems	**Rosemary**
6 cups	**Diced mixed vegetables**

Shake Up Pizza Night With These Unexpected Combos

Butternut Squash and Sage

Butternut squash and sage are a sublime combination. Thinly slice butternut squash into pepperoni-size rings and freeze dry. You can also freeze dry the sage. To make your pizza, rehydrate the squash and sage by adding warm water. Drizzle olive oil over the pizza crust, top with squash slices, sage leaves, and dollops of ricotta cheese (which you can also freeze dry). Bake at 350°F until the crust is brown and ricotta is warmed through. Drizzle again with olive oil before serving.

Strawberry, Bacon and Chicken

To make this surprisingly delicious pizza quickly, freeze dry sliced strawberries, cubed cooked chicken, and crumbled bacon. When you're ready to assemble your pie, rehydrate ingredients with a quick soak in warm water. Top your crust with the berries, chicken cubes, and bacon, then add sliced onion, cilantro, and blue cheese crumbles. Bake until the crust is brown and all ingredients are hot. Drizzle with balsamic vinegar just before serving.

Cantaloupe and Ricotta

This is a light, vegetarian-friendly pizza that makes a nice Sunday brunch entree. Thinly slice and freeze dry ripe cantaloupe. To rehydrate, add warm water or immerse in warm water for one minute. Top crust with a bright olive oil, cantaloupe slices, and ricotta cheese. Bake until brown, then add peppery arugula or cilantro leaves and a dash of olive oil before serving.

**Freeze-dried pizza makes a great snack.
Eat the pieces like you would eat your favorite crackers!**

Squash & Mozzarella Quiche

INSTRUCTIONS:

Preheat oven to 350ºF.

Sauté squash, zucchini, and thyme in olive oil for four minutes.

Whisk together milk, salt, pepper, egg powder, and water in a bowl until blended (may need to add extra water if using freeze-dried ingredients).

Layer sautéed squash on bottom, sprinkle with shredded mozzarella cheese, then pour in milk mixture.

Bake for 45 minutes. Garnish with diced shallots.

When cool, cut into squares.

INGREDIENTS

1	**Pie crust, fresh or store-bought**
2 cups	**Green or yellow squash, sliced (fresh or freeze dried)**
2 cups	**Zucchini, sliced (fresh or freeze dried)**
¼ cup	**Diced shallots**
1 Tbsp.	**Chopped thyme (fresh or freeze dried)**
1 cup	**2% milk**
1 tsp.	**Salt**
To taste	**Black pepper**
6 Tbsp.	**Raw egg powder + 6 tbs. water = 3 whole eggs**
¾ cup	**Shredded part-skim mozzarella cheese (fresh or freeze dried).**

Turkey Stuffing

CORNBREAD STUFFING (SOUTHERN STYLE)
Preheat the oven to 350°F.

Combine crumbled cornbread and stuffing ingredients in a large bowl.

Melt 1 stick of butter in a skillet and sauté the onion and celery until translucent. Add to the stuffing mixture. Melt the remaining stick of butter and combine with stock, eggs, and sage.

Add the cornbread and stuffing mixture and stir. Season with salt and pepper, pour into a greased pan, and bake uncovered about 45 minutes.

INGREDIENTS

SOUTHERN STYLE:	**Make 1 pan of your favorite cornbread, let set for two days.**
1 (14 oz.)	**Bag of herbed stuffing**
2 sticks	**Unsalted butter**
1 large	**Sweet onion, chopped**
1 cup	**Celery, chopped**
4-5 cups	**Turkey stock**
5 large	**Eggs**
1 Tbsp.	**Dried sage**

APPLE AND ONION STUFFING (NORTHERN STYLE)
Use the recipe above, except substitute bread crumbs for cornbread and add 2 diced apples to the mixture. Some northern recipes also call for 1 pound of seasoned pork sausage added just before baking.

SQUASH AND SOURDOUGH STUFFING (WEST COAST STYLE)
Use the recipe above, except substitute sourdough bread for the cornbread. Instead of apples, add diced squash, orange zest, and parsley (*pictured below*).

Curried Butternut Squash Salad

INSTRUCTIONS:

Roast diced butternut squash and onions with a sprinkle of salt, pepper, and curry powder, then toss them with diced apples, bananas, cashews, orzo, or quinoa, and a tablespoon of coconut flavored olive oil.

This pasta or quinoa salad freeze dries beautifully and tastes great on hot days.

Measure ingredients to personal preference.

INGREDIENTS

Butternut squash, diced

Onions, diced

Curry powder

Apples, diced

Bananas, diced

Cashews

Quinoa or orzo pasta

Coconut flavored olive oil

Salt and pepper

Tips For Using Freeze-Dried Herbs

CONVERTING FRESH HERB AMOUNTS TO FREEZE DRIED:

After they're freeze dried, the flavors of herbs will be more concentrated. A good guideline is to start with a third of the total amount of dried herbs the recipe calls for.

Give your dish a taste and see if it needs more. Strength of flavor can actually vary by plant so it's a good rule whether you're using fresh or freeze-dried herbs.

Salsa Fresca

INSTRUCTIONS:

Dice the onion, garlic, jalapeños, and tomatoes. Rough chop the cilantro and combine. Squeeze the juice from the lime over the mixture, add salt and stir.

Serve with chips, over fish, or on top of grilled crusty bread lightly rubbed with garlic.

INGREDIENTS

¼	**Onion**
1	**Garlic clove**
1	**Lime**
½ tsp.	**Salt**
1-2	**Jalapeño peppers**
4-6	**Plum tomatoes**
½ bunch	**Cilantro**

Flavored Powders

GREENS
Greens (like kale) can be freeze dried and then ground into a powder to add to smoothies or other recipes (like spaghetti sauce).

FRUITS
Powdered freeze-dried fruit adds flavor to things like frosting or baked goods. Powder the freeze-dried fruits and use the powder in cakes, muffins, pancakes and tarts.

MARSHMALLOWS
Grind up freeze-dried marshmallows to make marshmallow powder, which works great as a substitute for powdered sugar in most recipes while adding an alternate flavor.

HERBS AND PICKLES
Add flavors to your favorite recipes or snacks like popcorn and veggie chips.

Sweet Pepper Melange Powder

This makes the perfect spreadable topping for garlic bread.

INSTRUCTIONS:

Combine all ingredients in a large bowl and mix until evenly distributed. Freeze dry and pack in airtight containers.

Powder the mixture in a blender or food processor and add the powder to softened butter.

INGREDIENTS

4 cups	**Diced red, green, yellow and orange peppers (in any combination)**
1 medium	**Yellow onion**
1 tsp.	**Fresh oregano**
1 tsp.	**Fresh thyme**
½ tsp.	**Dried red pepper flakes**

LUNCH IDEAS

FREEZE DRY LUNCH MEATS AND CHEESE

Lunch meat and cheese roll-ups or sandwiches are a delicious way to send protein with your little ones or to take to work. Freeze drying lunch meat and cheese allows you to take advantage of bulk sales and eliminate trips to the grocery store.

To freeze dry deli slices of turkey, ham, or roast beef, roll the slices up like a sleeping bag and freeze dry in a single layer on trays.

To rehydrate, dip in cool water or spritz with water. You can tell by the look and feel when they are fully hydrated.

For lunches, freeze dry cracker-sized slices of cheese in a single layer on trays. To rehydrate, place in a ziplock bag with a damp paper towel and let freeze-dried cheese slowly come back to life. Some people love freeze-dried cheese without rehydrating because of its crunchy texture.

FREEZE-DRIED SIDES

Freeze-dried vegetables sprinkled with seasoning are also good lunchtime sides.

Vegetable chips are easy to make, don't have the unhealthy aspects of fried chips, and are the perfect way to sneak an extra serving of veggies into your day.

Yogurt drops are another lunch box favorite. They pack a ton of protein, have a creamy taste that kids love, and don't need refrigeration.

TRAIL MIX

Make your own trail mix for anytime on-the-go snacking with ingredients like freeze-dried fruit, chocolate chips, nuts or sunflower seeds.

HOT LUNCHES

If you have lunchtime access to a microwave or instant hot water machine, rehydrating meals just takes a minute. A few hot lunch ideas include:

- **CHILI WITH RED BEANS AND VEGETABLES**
- **MAC & CHEESE**
- **VEGETABLE OR MEAT LASAGNA**
- **SOUP OR STEW**

Guacamole To Go

INSTRUCTIONS:

Combine fresh avocados with your favorite guacamole ingredients and spread onto a tray. Freeze dry. Package in single servings. Rehydrate when ready to eat—anywhere, anytime. No refrigeration required!

Cinnamon Apple Slices

INSTRUCTIONS:

Slice apples into thin pieces and sprinkle with cinnamon and sugar. Freeze dry and serve as a crunchy snack.

Fruit & Nut Trail Mix

INSTRUCTIONS:

Freeze dry bananas and strawberries, then mix with almonds or pistachios and dried coconut. Divide into snack bag portions.

Breakfast Skillet

Makes 6 individual meals.

INSTRUCTIONS:

Stir-fry the vegetables for 2 minutes in 2 tablespoons of olive oil.

Add cooked and crumbled turkey or sausage and stir. Add eggs to mixture and scramble.

Freeze dry in individual packets.

Make a slice of whole grain toast while you boil water to rehydrate your meal.

INGREDIENTS

12	**Eggs**
2 Tbsp.	**Olive oil**
6 oz.	**Turkey or vegetarian sausage, cooked**
3 cups	**Peppers, onions and squash, chopped**
To taste	**Salt and pepper**

Oatmeal Apple Bites

These bites are great for a breakfast on the go or a mid-day snack.

Cook a batch of oatmeal and stir in apples that are sliced or diced to about 1". Place in bite-size dollops on the freeze dryer trays and run them through a standard cycle.

Pancakes With Powdered Fruit

INSTRUCTIONS:

In a bowl, sift together flour, strawberry powder, sugar, baking powder, and salt.

In another bowl, beat the eggs, milk, and vanilla.

While butter is melting on a griddle, combine wet and dry ingredients.

Ladle 1/4 cup of the batter onto the griddle (you can use a pancake mold if desired). Cook until bubbles break the surface.

Flip and cook about 1 minute more on the other side.

Repeat with remaining batter, adding butter to the skillet as needed.

INGREDIENTS

1½ cups	**All-purpose flour**
3 Tbsp.	**Sugar**
1 Tbsp.	**Baking powder**
¼ tsp.	**Salt**
2	**Large eggs**
1¼ cups	**Milk**
½ tsp.	**Vanilla extract**
2 Tbsp.	**Powdered freeze-dried strawberries**
3 Tbsp.	**Unsalted butter**

Add fruit powders such as bananas, raspberries, and blueberries to pancakes and waffle batters.

100% WHOLE FRUIT POWDER

Cornbread Muffins

This recipe is a perfect way to use freeze-dried corn.

INSTRUCTIONS:

Preheat oven to 400°F. Grease muffin pan or add muffin liners.

Combine dry ingredients in a large bowl.

In a separate bowl, combine egg and buttermilk. Add to dry ingredients and stir until just combined.

Spoon batter into prepared muffin cups.

Bake at 400°F for 15 to 20 minutes or until a toothpick inserted into a muffin comes out clean.

INGREDIENTS

½ cup	Freeze-dried corn, ground (or 1¼ cups freeze-dried corn, whole)
½ cup	All purpose flour
1 cup	Corn meal (finely ground)
1 tsp.	Salt
1½ tsp.	Baking powder
2 Tbsp.	Sugar
1 large	Egg
1¼ cup	Buttermilk
2 Tbsp.	Unsalted butter

Bran Muffins With Powdered Apples

You can also use other fruits such as pineapple, bananas, cherries, or blueberries.

INSTRUCTIONS:

Preheat oven to 375°F.

Sift together dry ingredients in a large bowl, then whisk together wet ingredients in another bowl.

Combine wet and dry ingredients and stir gently until just combined.

Coat muffin cups lightly with oil or insert paper baking cups.

Fill each cup half full.

Bake for 15–17 minutes or until toothpick comes out clean.

INGREDIENTS

½ cup +2 Tbsp.	**Whole wheat flour**
½ cup	**Oat bran**
3 Tbsp.	**Brown sugar**
1¼ tsp.	**Baking powder**
⅛ tsp.	**Baking soda**
Dash	**Salt**
¼ tsp.	**Ground cinnamon**
⅛ tsp.	**Ground nutmeg**
1	**Egg white**
½ cup	**Buttermilk**
1 Tbsp.	**Canola oil**
1	**Powdered freeze-dried apple**

Blueberry Muffins

INSTRUCTIONS:

Preheat oven to 375°F. Beat butter and sugar together, add eggs, milk, and vanilla. Beat well. Set aside.

Mix dry ingredients (except blueberries). Set aside.

Combine the wet ingredients with the dry, being careful not to overmix. Fold in freeze-dried blueberries and let sit for a few minutes to soften. Grease muffin tin or use liners. Fill each one about 3/4 full.

Bake for 25-30 minutes (or until toothpick inserted in center comes out clean). Remove from pan and let cool.

INGREDIENTS

2 cups	**All-purpose flour**
½ cup	**Butter**
1½ tsp.	**Baking powder**
¾ cup	**Freeze-dried or fresh blueberries**
½ tsp.	**Salt**
¾ cup	**Sugar**
2	**Eggs**
¾ cup	**Milk**
1 tsp.	**Vanilla extract**

Leftover Pie Bites

You can turn leftover pie into a scrumptious freeze-dried treat! Simply take each pie and mash each one separately so the crust and the filling look more like a dough. (Note: You can also make cream pies too, like chocolate silk, banana cream, or coconut cream.) Then, scoop the dough-like mixture using a small ice cream scoop/melon baller and place on parchment-lined freeze dryer trays. When complete, these yummy cookie-like treats can be eaten immediately or stored for the next time you're craving your favorite pie.

Strawberry Chocolate Chip Cookies

Makes 3-4 dozen cookies.

INSTRUCTIONS:

Preheat oven to 350°F.

Whisk together flour, baking soda, and salt.

In a separate bowl, cream together butter and sugar. Mix in eggs, one at a time. Add vanilla and honey. Gradually blend in dry ingredients. Mix in freeze-dried strawberries and chocolate chips. Drop by tablespoonful onto baking sheet.

Bake for 10 to 11 minutes or until cookies begin to brown. Bake an extra 1 to 2 minutes for a crisper cookie.

Cool for 2 minutes on baking sheet. Move to wire rack to cool completely.

INGREDIENTS

2½ cups	All-purpose flour
1 ½ tsp.	Baking soda
½ tsp.	Salt
½ cup	Brown sugar
½ cup	Butter, room temperature
2	Large eggs
2 tsp.	Vanilla extract
1 Tbsp.	Honey
2¼ cups	Freeze-dried strawberries
1 cup	Chocolate chips

VARIATION: MARSHMALLOW CHOCOLATE CHIP COOKIES

Make your regular chocolate chip cookie recipe, but chill the dough for about an hour in the fridge. When the dough has chilled, roll into balls, and make a hole in the center of each ball with the large end of a chopstick. Insert two freeze-dried marshmallows in each hole, pinch to seal the hole, and bake as normal. The result is a marshmallow-filled chocolate chip cookie!

You can also add marshmallows to your regular chocolate chip or double chocolate cookie dough recipe and bake like normal to give it a gooey marshmallow flavor.

Rhubarb Bread

A crunchy top with a sweet and nutty inside.

INSTRUCTIONS:

Preheat oven to 350ºF.

In a bowl, mix together the brown sugar, oil, egg, buttermilk, and vanilla.

In a separate bowl, mix the dry ingredients for the bread.

To the dry ingredients, fold in 2 cups of freeze-dried rhubarb that has been rehydrated and drained. Fold in 1 1/2 cups nuts.

Combine wet and dry ingredients and stir until incorporated.

Pour into three small loaf pans or two medium-size loaf pans that have been greased and floured.

Crumble the topping on top of each loaf.

Bake at 350ºF for 40 to 45 minutes.

TO REHYDRATE THE RHUBARB: Cover the dry rhubarb with water and let it absorb the water for about 5 minutes.
Drain well.

INGREDIENTS

Bread:

1½ cups	**Brown sugar**
⅔ cup	**Oil**
1	**Egg**
1 cup	**Buttermilk**
1 tsp.	**Vanilla**
2½ cups	**Flour**
1 tsp.	**Salt**
1 tsp.	**Baking soda**
2 cups	**Fresh or freeze-dried rhubarb that is rehydrated and drained**
1 ½ cups	**Nuts**

Topping:

⅓ cup	**Sugar**
1 Tbsp.	**Soft butter**

MAKE-AHEAD PARTY FOOD

SAVE TIME AND REDUCE STRESS BY PRE-MAKING, THEN FREEZE DRYING, APPETIZERS AND SNACKS FOR YOUR NEXT PARTY.

APPETIZERS:

One-bite versions of sliders, meatballs, mini crab cakes, and crustless mini quiches provide delicious protein anchors for other appetizers. Place cooked or uncooked meatballs, mini burgers, crab cakes or quiche on trays and freeze dry. Store in airtight containers or Mylar bags until you're ready to use. To reconstitute, just add water. If you've freeze dried your snacks uncooked, once you rehydrate, they'll be ready to bake or grill.

DIPS AND SPREADS:

Spinach and artichoke dip, tapenade, queso, and bean dips are all popular party foods that are easy to serve with bread. To freeze dry spreads and dips, spread a layer on the tray and freeze dry. Store in airtight containers or Mylar bags until you're ready to use. To reconstitute, just add small amounts of warm water until it reaches the original consistency.

One of the easiest party snacks is guacamole. You can freeze dry your favorite avocados and simply break them into pieces and mix with water. As the avocados rehydrate, they turn into a delicious guacamole dip. Serve with a bag of your favorite chips and enjoy!

On the day of the party, slice fresh bread and put out crackers for dipping.

Berry Smoothie

INSTRUCTIONS:

Freeze dry your favorite berries like strawberries, blueberries, raspberries, or blackberries. Crush into a powder and combine each berry equally together.

Mix 3 tablespoons of powder mixture into 1 cup of milk. Stir and serve.

Green Smoothie

INSTRUCTIONS:

Chop kale, broccoli, and pineapple into bite-size pieces and place on trays. You can freeze dry all of these ingredients at once.

After freeze drying, combine kale, broccoli, and pineapple in a 1:1:1 ratio, then chop by hand or in a food processor until coarse.

When you're ready for your smoothie, combine 1 cup of the mixture with 1 cup of ice and 3/4 cup of milk, nut milk or yogurt in a blender. For a dose of protein, add 1/4 cup of almonds.

Smoothie Bites

A unique freeze-dried version of a smoothie can be made into delicious dry bites!

Mix fruit into a slurry and add yogurt. Freeze dry in molds, then enjoy as a crunchy freeze-dried snack!

Raspberry, Blueberry & Yogurt

Açai Berry & Yogurt

Blueberry Greek Yogurt Smoothie

INSTRUCTIONS:

Blend ingredients together with ice to your liking and enjoy!

INGREDIENTS

½ cup	**Plain Greek yogurt**
¼ cup	**Freeze-dried banana**
½ cup	**Freeze-dried blueberries**
1 Tbsp.	**Freeze-dried spinach, powdered**
½ cup	**Unsweetened almond milk**
	Ice

Tangy Lemonade

INSTRUCTIONS:

Lemons can be sliced and freeze dried with the rind on or peeled and freeze dried without the peel.

When you're ready to make lemonade, pour cold water over the freeze-dried slices, and add sugar until it reaches your desired flavor.

INGREDIENTS

Freeze-dried lemons

Sugar

TRAVEL SNACKS

SAVE MONEY AND ENJOY NUTRITIOUS SNACKS ON THE GO WITHOUT HAVING TO RELY ON CONVENIENCE STORES OR AIRPORT OPTIONS.

SWEET & SPICY BANANA CHIPS
These chips satisfy your salty/sweet cravings, but keep you away from high-fat snacks. Freeze dry thinly sliced bananas with olive oil, and add a dash of sea salt and freshly cracked black pepper.

SPICY CHICKPEAS
To make this addictive snack, combine drained and rinsed chickpeas with olive oil, paprika, salt, and garlic powder before freeze drying.

APPLE, ORANGE AND ONION MIX
If you haven't tried this odd combination, you're in for a surprise. Before freeze drying, we recommend testing the ratio of apples, oranges, and onions that you prefer. When you're ready, slice apples, oranges, and sweet onions into 1/2 cubes and mix together before freeze drying.

CHILI
Freeze dry your favorite chili (or soup) recipe for an instant comfort-food meal. If you're feeling like a treat, pick up a bag of corn chips to top your chili.

MAPLE APPLE CHIPS
We like these for breakfast with freeze-dried yogurt cubes. Combine thin apple slices with a pinch of salt and a drizzle of olive oil and maple syrup.

YOGURT CUBES OR DROPS
Freeze dry yogurt by pouring it into an even layer on the pan or by pouring it in silicone molds. Process as usual. Yogurt drops can be made by squeezing out yogurt in dollops from a pastry bag onto trays.

BASIL & SQUASH CHIPS
Slice any kind of cooked squash into 1/4" rounds and place on trays. Also, place fresh basil leaves on trays. When they're done freeze drying, crumble the basil and toss the chips with sea salt and the basil. Divide into snack bags.

Chapter 7
Quick Recipes Using Freeze Dried Food

Using Freeze-Dried Ingredients

The following recipes specifically make use of your already freeze-dried food. Prepare these recipes for a quick dinner, a delicious on-the-go meal for the trail, for use in an emergency, or just because.

The results are just as delicious and nutritious as when prepared with fresh ingredients!

Garden Stew

Makes 4-6 servings.

Combine all ingredients into a bag or bowl. Add 5 cups hot water.

TO REHYDRATE:
Add hot water and allow 10-20 minutes to rehydrate. Stir occasionally. Add more hot water to taste and desired consistency.

INGREDIENTS

3 cups	**Freeze-dried black beans**
3 cups	**Freeze-dried squash or zucchini (cubed)**
3 cups	**Freeze-dried corn**
5 tsp.	**Chicken or vegetable bouillon**
5 tsp.	**Freeze-dried onions (diced)**
1 tsp.	**Garlic powder**
To taste	**Salt and pepper**

Ideas For Using Freeze-Dried Apples

SLICED FOR PIE – To freeze dry apples for pies, peel and slice them less than 1" thick, freeze dry them in a single layer on the trays, then store in an airtight container with an oxygen absorber until you're ready to use them.

DICED FOR GRANOLA AND YOGURT – Freeze-dried apples are delicious and wonderfully crunchy. To use as a crunchy topping, dice apples with the nutritious peel on and freeze dry.

DICED FOR QUICK BREADS AND SPICE MUFFINS - Add to your favorite baked recipes.

RINGED FOR HOT DRINKS – Peel your apples and slice thinly, freeze dry in a single layer on trays, and store in an airtight container with an oxygen absorber. Float rings of freeze-dried apples in your holiday hot ciders and spiced punches. As they rehydrate, they'll soak up the spicy flavors, making a delicious decoration.

SLICED FOR SNACKS – If desired, sprinkle with cinnamon, brown sugar, or your favorite pie spice before freeze drying . Try them with salty, buttered popcorn on movie night.

Bean and Cheese Burrito

INSTRUCTIONS:

Combine all freeze dried ingredients in a bag.

Package tortilla separately.

Add enough hot water to the dried ingredients. Start with 1/2 cup. Stir occasionally. Once rehydrated, spread on tortilla.

This is perfect to take backpacking or camping.

INGREDIENTS

1	**Flour tortilla**
¼ cup	**Freeze-dried black beans**
⅛ cup	**Freeze-dried tomatoes**
⅛ cup	**Freeze-dried shredded cheese**
⅛ cup	**Freeze-dried corn**
¼ tsp.	**Taco seasoning**
¼ tsp.	**Freeze-dried cilantro**

Egg and Vegetable Scramble

Makes 1 serving.

INSTRUCTIONS:

Combine all ingredients in a dish.

To rehydrate, add 1/3 to 1/4 cup hot water.

Once rehydrated, pour onto hot skillet or pan and cook like scrambled eggs.

INGREDIENTS

4 Tbsp.	**Raw freeze-dried egg**
⅛ cup	**Freeze-dried bell pepper**
⅛ cup	**Freeze-dried tomatoes**
¼ tsp.	**Garlic powder**
¼ tsp.	**Onion powder**
To taste	**Salt and pepper**

Island Haystacks

Makes 4-6 servings.

INSTRUCTIONS:

Combine all ingredients in a dish.

Add enough boiling water to cover food. Start with 5 cups. Stir well and wait to rehydrate.

INGREDIENTS

3 cups	**Freeze-dried rice**
3 cups	**Freeze-dried ham (diced)**
1½ cup	**Freeze-dried pineapple**
1½ cup	**Freeze-dried peas**
½ cup	**Freeze-dried bell pepper**
1 tsp.	**Ginger**
1 tsp.	**Garlic**
½ tsp.	**Cumin**
½ tsp.	**Five-spice powder**
3 tsp.	**Vegetable bouillon**

Sweet & Spicy Chicken & Rice

Makes 4-6 servings.

INSTRUCTIONS:

Place freeze-dried ingredients in a bowl and rehydrate with 5 cups boiling water. Add 2 cups of your favorite salsa.

Keep adding salsa until food is fully rehydrated and reaches desired consistency.

INGREDIENTS

3 cups	**Freeze-dried rice**
2 cups	**Freeze-dried black beans**
1 cup	**Freeze-dried chicken (cubed and cooked)**
1 cup	**Freeze-dried banana slices**
½ cup	**Freeze-dried pineapple**
2 cups	**Fresh salsa**

Potato & Vegetable Soup Mix

Makes 4-6 servings.

INGREDIENTS

3 cups	**Mashed potato flakes**
3 cups	**Freeze-dried vegetables (any vegetable mix will work)**
3 tsp.	**Dried chives**
½ cup	**Freeze-dried milk powder**
4 tsp.	**Chicken or vegetable bouillon**
1 tsp.	**Salt**
To taste	**Pepper**

INSTRUCTIONS:

Combine all ingredients.

Add 6 cups of hot water. Stir well.

Add more water to taste and desired consistency.

Tomato Soup with Grilled Cheese Croutons

INSTRUCTIONS:

Rehydrate tomato soup with hot water.

Add freeze-dried grilled cheese sandwich cubes, and enjoy them crunchy or allow to rehydrate in the soup.

CROUTONS:

Lightly butter bread and grill your sandwiches in a skillet until the cheese is melted.

Allow sandwiches to cool on a rack until cheese is solid. Cut crusts off the sandwiches, then cut into 9 squares. Place squares in one layer on freeze dryer trays and process. Keep croutons in an air-tight container with an oxygen absorber until ready to serve.

Place freeze-dried croutons directly into hot soup to serve.

THE CHEESE:

For even more flavor impact, don't limit your cheese to just cheddar. For best results, slice the soft cheeses and shred the harder varieties (no processed cheese). Here are some of our favorite combinations:

GOUDA & MEDIUM CHEDDAR

SHARP CHEDDAR & SWISS

GRUYÈRE & PROVOLONE

RICOTTA & RACLETTE

BLUE CHEESE & FETA

BLUE CHEESE & PEPPER JACK

FLAVORED OR HERBED GOAT CHEESE

MUENSTER & FONTINA

Join an online community of fellow freeze drying fanatics

There are several large groups on social media full of loyal freeze dryer owners just waiting for you to join. Here are just a few of them:

"Betty's Harvest Right Freeze Dryers Group" on Facebook

"Harvest Right Freeze Dryers – Freeze Drying Adventures" on Facebook

"Retired at 40 – Live. Life. Simple" on YouTube and Facebook

Chapter 8

Recipes & Tips:
Featured Fans

Zucchini Fritters *(Kim Kane)*

Note: You can rehydrate the zucchini and make these fresh, or you can make them fresh and then freeze dry.

INSTRUCTIONS:

If using fresh shredded zucchini, place in a colander set over a bowl, and sprinkle the zucchini lightly with salt. Allow the zucchini to stand for 10 minutes. Using your hands, squeeze out as much liquid from the zucchini as possible. Transfer the zucchini to a large bowl.

If using freeze dried, place zucchini in a colander and spray with warm water while gently stirring. They only take a minute or two to rehydrate. Then pat dry with a paper towel. Transfer the zucchini to a large bowl.

Add the flour, eggs, onions, salt, and pepper to the bowl, stirring until the mixture is combined. Line a plate with paper towels.

Add the olive oil to a large sauté pan set over medium heat. Once the oil is hot, scoop 3 tablespoon-size mounds of the zucchini mixture into the pan, pressing them lightly into rounds and spacing them at least 2 inches apart. Cook the zucchini fritters for 2 to 3 minutes, then flip them once and cook an additional 2 minutes until golden brown and cooked throughout.

Transfer the zucchini fritters to the paper towel-lined plate and immediately sprinkle them with salt. Repeat the scooping and cooking process with the remaining zucchini mixture. Serve with ranch dressing or sour cream.

TO FREEZE DRY: Pat off excess oil with a paper towel and place them on fresh paper towels on your freeze dryer trays.

TO REHYDRATE: Wrap the fritters in moist paper towels for 10 minutes. Add more time as needed. Place in the oven at 350°F for 10 minutes to heat back up.

INGREDIENTS:

4 cups	**Fresh shredded zucchini (or 6 cups freeze dried)**
⅔ cup	**All-purpose flour or Bisquick**
2 large	**Eggs, lightly beaten**
⅓ cup	**Minced onions**
¼ tsp.	**Salt**
⅛ tsp.	**Pepper**
2 Tbsp.	**Olive oil**

Optional: Sour cream or ranch dressing for serving

Find more tips and recipes on Facebook at 'Harvest Right Freeze Dryers – Freeze Drying Adventures'.

Potato Casserole / Kugela *(Kim Kane)*

INSTRUCTIONS:

Preheat oven to 375°F.

Grease a 9x13 inch baking dish.

In a large skillet over medium heat, fry bacon pieces until crisp; remove to paper towels.

Reserve half of the bacon drippings and set aside.

Return skillet to stove. Stir onions and cook until soft and translucent.

In a large bowl, stir together reserved drippings, bacon, onion, and potatoes.

Mix in flour, milk, and eggs.

Season with salt and pepper to taste.

INGREDIENTS

1 lb.	**Bacon diced and cooked well (Once cooked, absorb as much grease as possible. For a longer shelf-life, you could use turkey bacon.)**
1 large	**Onion, grated**
10 cups	**Rehydrated freeze-dried shredded potatoes**
½ cup	**Flour**
12 oz.	**Milk**
6	**Eggs**
To taste	**Salt and pepper**

Pour into baking dish and bake in a preheated oven until top is nicely brown, about 1 hour.

Cut into squares and serve with sour cream, or cut into 1/2" slices and freeze dry.

TO REHYDRATE:

Wrap freeze-dried slices in wet paper towels and place in a zip-close plastic bag. Wait 10 minutes and check for doneness. If not quite soft, check in 5-minute increments.

Another option is to place them in a bowl of hot water, and gently turn after a few minutes. Once rehydrated, pat dry and place in the oven at 325°F for approximately 5 minutes to reheat.

Ritz Casserole *(Kim Kane)*

INSTRUCTIONS:

Preheat oven to 400°F.

Lightly spray an 8 × 8 baking dish with oil.

In a large mixing bowl, combine your cooked and shredded chicken, soup, Parmesan, mushrooms, spinach, stock, Italian seasoning and a generous pinch of salt and pepper. Spread this mixture out in your prepared baking dish. Sprinkle mozzarella cheese on top of your casserole and sprinkle on crushed Ritz crackers. Drizzle melted butter over everything.

Pop the casserole in the oven and bake 18-20 minutes, or until the sides are bubbly and the crackers lightly browned.

TO FREEZE DRY: Bake first, then freeze dry.

TO REHYDRATE: For every 1 ounce of casserole, add 3 ounces of boiling water.

Stir well, cover, and let sit 15 minutes. Check occasionally to stir. If needed, add more water.

To reheat, you can use the same method of baking as indicated above.

INGREDIENTS:

1 lb.	**Cooked and shredded chicken**
1 can (10 oz.)	**Cream of mushroom soup**
1 cup	**Grated Parmesan cheese**
approx. 1 cup	**Chopped mushrooms**
1 box (10 oz.)	**Frozen spinach, defrosted, with excess water squeezed out**
½ cup	**Chicken stock or water**
1½ Tbsp.	**Italian seasoning**
	Salt and pepper to taste
1 cup	**Grated mozzarella cheese**
1 sleeve	**Ritz crackers, lightly crushed**
4 Tbsp.	**Butter, melted**

Potato Pancakes/Latkes *(Kim Kane)*

INSTRUCTIONS.

Rehydrate 4 cups of shredded freeze dried potatoes.

In a large bowl, combine potatoes with eggs, flour, and 1 teaspoon salt.

Over medium heat, use a large skillet and heat about 1/8" oil until shimmering. To test if oil is hot enough, sprinkle with some flour. If flour bubbles and dissolves immediately, oil is ready.

Add a few spoonfuls of potato mixture to the oil. Pat down to flatten. Fry until crispy and golden, about 3 minutes per side.

Transfer to paper towels to drain, then sprinkle with remaining salt.

Serve with applesauce or sour cream.

Note: You can use fresh grated potatoes and then freeze dry your leftovers. Pat off excess oil and freeze dry on paper towels.

TO REHYDRATE:

Wrap freeze-dried latkes in wet paper towels and place in a zip-close plastic bag. Wait 10 minutes and check for doneness. If not quite soft, check in 5-minute increments. Another option is to place them in a bowl of hot water and gently turn after a few minutes.

Once rehydrated, pat dry and place in the oven at 325°F for approximately 5 minutes to reheat.

INGREDIENTS

4 cups	**Rehydrated shredded freeze-dried potatoes, well drained (It's always best to pat dry with paper towels.)**
2	**Large eggs, beaten**
½ cup	**All-purpose flour**
1 ½ tsp.	**Kosher salt, divided**
2 Tbsp.	**Freshly chopped chives or onions that have been sautéed**

Canola oil for frying

Applesauce or sour cream for serving

Cuban Black Beans and Rice *(Kim Kane)*

INGREDIENTS

Beans:

1¼ cups	**Dried black beans, rinsed**
10 cups	**Water**
1 medium	**Onion, halved**
1 medium	**Green bell pepper (cored), halved**
1	**Cubanelle pepper (cored), halved**

Rice:

2 cups	**Long-grain rice**
1 Tbsp.	**Extra-virgin olive oil**
4 oz.	**Slab or thick-cut bacon, diced**
1 medium	**Yellow onion, finely chopped**
1 medium	**Green bell pepper (cored), finely chopped**
1 tsp.	**Ground cumin**
1 tsp.	**Dried oregano**
1	**Bay leaf**
2 tsp.	**Sherry vinegar (may substitute white distilled vinegar)**
To taste	**Salt to taste**

INSTRUCTIONS:

1. Place the beans in a 4- to 5-quart heavy pot along with the water, onion, green bell pepper, and cubanelle pepper. Bring to boil over high heat, then reduce the heat to medium and cook, uncovered, for 1 hour 40 minutes to 2 hours, maintaining gentle bubbling, until the beans are tender yet still retain their shape. (Test the beans for doneness; the range in time depends somewhat on how fresh the beans are.) Drain, reserving 4 cups of the cooking liquid. Discard the vegetables used for flavoring; the yield of beans is 2 cups. Or, just use 2 cans of beans.

2. Rinse and drain beans well. Set aside.

3. Heat the oil in the same pot over medium heat. Add the diced bacon and cook for about 3 minutes, until golden. Add the onion, green bell pepper, cumin, oregano, and bay leaf; cook for about 5 minutes, until the onion has softened.

4. Add the rice and stir to coat thoroughly. Add the beans and their reserved cooking liquid, the sherry vinegar, and salt. Stir well, then taste for seasoning; add a dash more vinegar, cumin, oregano and/or salt as needed. The liquid should be flavorful. Cook, uncovered, for 8 to 12 minutes, until most of the liquid has been absorbed and small holes have formed on the surface of the rice. Fluff the rice with a fork, reduce the heat to the lowest setting, cover tightly, and cook for 20 minutes.

5. Remove from heat, uncover, and let stand for at least 10 minutes before serving. Discard the bay leaf.

PREPPING FOR REHYDRATING:

Remember to keep everything chopped small so it rehydrates as fast as the rice does.

Black Bean & Sausage Soup *(Kim Kane)*

INSTRUCTIONS:

Brown the sausage, drain, then pat off excess grease with paper towels and set aside.

Heat oil in a large pot over medium heat. Add onion and garlic; cook 5 minutes, stirring occasionally.

Stir in beans, sausage, broth, chili powder, oregano, peppers, and cumin.

Simmer, covered, 60 minutes or until beans are tender. Add sausage during last 30 minutes of cooking.

Remove about 3 cups of the mixture to a blender and puree; return to pot.

Add cheese and stir until melted.

Serve with sour cream and tortilla chips.

TO FREEZE DRY: Fill trays with the appropriate weight for your machine.

TO REHYDRATE: For each ounce of soup, add 4 ounces of boiling water. Cover and let simmer until everything is soft. Start checking after around 20 minutes. Add more water as needed.

INGREDIENTS

4 cans	**Black beans**
2 Tbsp.	**Vegetable oil**
2 lbs.	**Sweet Italian sausage, casings removed, crumbled**
1 large	**Onion, chopped**
4 cloves	**Garlic**
12 cups	**Chicken broth**
4 tsp.	**Chili powder**
3 tsp.	**Dried oregano**
4 tsp.	**Cumin**
3	**Sweet red peppers, cored, seeded and chopped**
2 cups	**Shredded cheese of your choice**

Optional: Hot sauce or crushed red pepper to taste

Chicken and Dumplings *(Kim Kane)*

INSTRUCTIONS:

Directions for Broth:

Put the chicken and veggies in a large pot, cover with water, and simmer, uncovered, until the chicken meat falls off of the bones (skim off foam every so often).

Remove the chicken and strain the broth.

Note: If you do not have a fat separator, leave the broth in the fridge overnight and remove the fat cap in the morning.

Pick the meat off the bones and finely chop and shred. Return broth and chicken to the pot.

Season the broth with salt, pepper, and chicken bouillon to taste.

Directions for Dumplings:

In a bowl, whisk flour, baking powder, and salt. In another bowl, whisk milk and melted butter until blended. Add to flour mixture. Stir just until moistened (do not overmix).

INGREDIENTS

Broth:

1	**Whole chicken (3 lbs.)**
4	**Carrots**
4	**Celery stalks**
1	**Large onion**
	Water to cover
To taste	**Salt & pepper**
1 tsp.	**Chicken bouillon granules (optional)**

Dumplings:

1⅓ cups	**All-purpose flour**
2 tsp.	**Baking powder**
¾ tsp.	**Salt**
⅔ cup	**2% milk**
1 Tbsp.	**Butter, melted**

Drop by rounded tablespoonfuls onto a parchment-lined baking sheet; set aside. You can also use a prepared baking mix, like Bisquick.

Drop dumplings into simmering soup, a few at a time. Reduce heat to low; cook, covered, 15-18 minutes or until a toothpick inserted in the center of dumplings comes out clean (do not lift cover while simmering).

TO FREEZE DRY: Cut the dumplings into no more than 1/2" bites. Distribute the dumplings evenly over your trays, and then do the same with the remaining broth, always ensuring you keep the weight within the tolerance for your machine.

TO REHYDRATE: For each ounce of soup, add 4 ounces of boiling water. Gently stir so as not to break up the dumplings. Cover and let simmer until everything is soft. Start checking after about 10 minutes. Add more water as needed.

15 Bean Soup *(Kim Kane)*

INSTRUCTIONS:

NOTE: *If making your own broth, use 3 ham hocks or 1 ham bone. Once done, let broth sit in the fridge until you can remove the fat cap since freeze drying fat does not work well.*

Open the beans, and set the flavor package aside.

Pour the beans into a large bowl, and sort any unwanted debris. Soak beans for 8 hours and drain.

While the beans are draining, sauté the onions in a large stockpot until translucent.

Add the broth, beans, diced tomatoes, lemon juice, and all the spices. Simmer until the beans are soft. Salt and pepper to taste.

INGREDIENTS

8 cups	Ham broth, or you can use water, beef, or vegetable broth
1	Package 15 bean soup
1	Onion, diced
2 cloves	Garlic
2 tsp.	Chili powder or to taste
1 can (15 oz.)	Diced tomatoes (or a quart of home canned)
2	Lemons, juiced
2 lbs.	Ham, diced (the leaner the better)

Optional: Hot sauce or crushed red pepper to taste

TO REHYDRATE: For each ounce of soup, add 4 ounces of boiling water. Cover and let simmer until everything is soft.

Add more water as needed.

Kim's Cream of Mushroom Soup *(Kim Kane)*

INSTRUCTIONS:

Clean one pound of mushrooms, remove stems, and set aside. Thinly slice the caps.

In a 4-quart sauce pan, sauté the sliced caps in the lemon juice and butter until soft. Remove mushrooms and set aside.

Sauté the onion and stems in the leftover juice until tender.

Stir in flour and cook for one minute, stirring constantly.

Gradually stir in the chicken broth, stirring constantly until thickened.

Blend contents of the pot with either an immersion blender or in batches in your blender.

Return to pot, stir in salt, pepper, milk, and mushrooms. Heat to a medium simmer.

INGREDIENTS

1 lb.	**Fresh mushrooms**
4 Tbsp.	**Butter**
1 tsp.	**Lemon juice**
1 small	**Onion, diced**
⅓ cup	**All-purpose flour**
3½ cups	**Chicken broth**
1 cup	**Whole milk**
To taste	**Salt and pepper**

TO REHYDRATE:

Concentrated- For every 1 ounce of freeze-dried soup use 2 ounces of boiling water.

Soup- For every 1 ounce of freeze-dried soup, use 4 ounces of boiling water.

Stir well, cover, and let simmer for 10 minutes. Check occasionally to stir and, if needed, add more water.

Tip: Brown some rehydrated pork chops and pour this over them for the gravy and simmer. Serve over mashed potatoes.

Rehydrated Mashed Potatoes *(Kim Kane)*

Note: Before freeze drying, peel and cook your potatoes and mash with milk. A little butter will not hurt, but the more you add, the shorter the shelf life. You can add the butter when you rehydrate them.

STOVE-TOP INSTRUCTIONS

Heat water to boiling, then add butter and salt.

Remove from heat and add cold milk.

Add the potatoes and onions. Stir gently. Fluff with a fork; do not whip.

Let sit for 2-3 minutes to thicken before serving.

MICROWAVE INSTRUCTIONS:

Combine water, butter, salt, and milk in a large microwave-safe bowl or dish.

Microwave on high for approximately 3 minutes. Remove from microwave and add the freeze-dried potatoes. Fluff with a fork; do not whip.

Before serving, let sit for 2-3 minutes to thicken. Serve with a little ranch dressing or sour cream.

INGREDIENTS

1½ cups	**Water**
2 Tbsp.	**Butter**
½ tsp.	**Salt**
½ cup	**Cold milk**
1⅓ cups	**Freeze-dried powdered potatoes**

Optional: sour cream or ranch dressing for serving

Chicken Broccoli Divan *(Kim Kane)*

INSTRUCTIONS:

Place the broccoli and chicken in a large baking dish.

Combine soup, sour cream, and milk in a small bowl and stir. Pour the soup mixture over the broccoli and chicken. Sprinkle with the cheese. Stir the bread crumbs and butter in a small bowl. Sprinkle the bread crumb mixture over the cheese.

Bake at 450°F for 20 minutes or until the chicken mixture is hot and bubbling.

TO FREEZE DRY: Baking before freeze drying is optional. If you do not bake it first, follow the baking directions once you rehydrate.

TO REHYDRATE: For every 1 ounce of freeze-dried divan, use 3 ounces of boiling water to rehydrate.

Cover with boiling water, stir well, and let sit. Check occasionally to stir and add more water if needed. Once rehydrated, you can eat as-is or place in a baking dish covered with the bread crumbs and butter. Bake at 450°F for 20 minutes or until the chicken mixture is hot and bubbling.

INGREDIENTS

4 cups	**Cooked broccoli florets, diced**
4 cups	**Cooked boneless, skinless chicken breast or turkey, cubed (shredded is even better)**
3 cans	**Condensed cream of chicken soup**
1 cup	**Milk**
1 cup	**Sour cream**
1 cup	**Shredded cheddar cheese**
½ cup	**Shredded parmesan**
4 Tbsp.	**Panko bread crumbs**
2 Tbsp.	**Butter, melted**
To taste	**Salt and pepper**

Hash Brown Patty Casserole Bake (Kim Kane)

This can be served as a side dish, or add diced lean ham for a main dish.

INSTRUCTIONS:

Preheat oven to 400°F.

Heat large skillet on medium-high heat. Add 1 tablespoon of oil. After oil is hot, cook hash browns for a few minutes on both sides so they're crispy. Remove from pan and set aside.

In same pan on medium-high heat, add remaining 1 tablespoon of oil. Add onions, bell peppers, and sausage. Break up sausage and add garlic powder, onion powder, salt, and pepper. Cook until sausage is browned. Set meat mixture aside.

In a bowl, beat together the milk and eggs.

Spray 9 x 9 pan with oil spray. Layer hash browns on bottom of pan. Cut them in half if needed to cover the bottom of the pan. It's okay if they're layered on top of each other.

Sprinkle 3/4 cup of cheese on top of hash browns. Pour meat mixture on top of the cheese. Pour the egg/milk mixture over the whole dish. Spread everything evenly. Sprinkle remaining cheese on top.

Bake uncovered at 400°F for about 20-25 minutes or until the egg is set and cheese is browned on top. Allow to cool a bit before serving.

INGREDIENTS

6	Hash brown patties, thawed
2 Tbsp.	Oil, divided
½	Onion, minced
1	Bell pepper, seeded & diced
½ lb.	Uncooked breakfast sausage
½ tsp.	Garlic powder
½ tsp.	Onion powder
½ tsp.	Salt
¼ tsp.	Black pepper
1 cup	Shredded cheddar cheese, divided
1 cup	Milk
5 large	Eggs

TO FREEZE DRY: Cut into serving-size portions and place on the trays. The other option is to cut the casserole into bite-size pieces and spread evenly on the tray.

TO REHYDRATE: If you used the serving-size portions, you can wrap them in wet paper towels and then place in a ziplock bag. Let them sit in the fridge for a few hours. If they are not quite done when you are ready to use, place them carefully in a container of hot water until done. Drain and pat dry when done. Heat back up in a 325°F oven for 10-15 minutes.

If you used the bite-size version, add 3 ounces of boiling water for every ounce of casserole. Spread over an oven-safe dish and use the same option as above to heat back up.

Carnitas *(Kim Kane)*

This is great served with soft shell tacos and all the fixings. It is also perfect for nachos.

INSTRUCTIONS:

Trim excess fat from pork butt; cut pork into 2" cubes and transfer to a bowl.

Combine salt, oregano, cumin, black pepper, chili powder, and paprika together in a bowl. Rub pork cubes with spice mixture. Coat seasoned pork cubes lightly in olive oil; place in pressure cooker. Cover pork cubes with orange juice, onion, and garlic.

Place lid on pressure cooker and lock; bring to full pressure over medium heat until pork is no longer pink in the center; about 60 minutes. Let pressure come down naturally, approximately 15 minutes.

Remove pork from pressure cooker and shred the meat.

TO FREEZE DRY: Line your trays with paper towels and freeze dry.

TO REHYDRATE: Place the amount of meat you want to rehydrate in a pot with a lid, and barely cover the meat with boiling water. Cover and simmer on the stove using the lowest setting for 5 minutes. You may need to add more water as you go. Once the meat is rehydrated, drain and place in a hot pan to quickly crisp it back up, stirring constantly.

INGREDIENTS

1 (6 lb.)	**Pork butt roast**
1½ Tbsp.	**Salt**
1 Tbsp.	**Dried oregano**
2 tsp.	**Ground cumin**
1 tsp.	**Ground black pepper**
½ tsp.	**Chili powder**
½ tsp.	**Paprika**
2 Tbsp. (or to taste)	**Olive oil**
1 cup	**Orange juice**
1	**Onion, coarsely chopped**
4 cloves (or to taste)	**Garlic, diced**

Spicy Chicken Thighs (Kim Kano)

INSTRUCTIONS:

Cut chicken thighs into small, bite-sized pieces. Remove any fat. Sprinkle the chicken with salt and pepper. Heat the oil in a large oven-proof skillet over medium-high heat.

Add the chicken and cook until browned. Transfer the chicken to a plate.

Reduce the heat to medium, add the onion, garlic, and red pepper flakes. Cook until the onions are soft, about 7 minutes.

Add the tomato paste and stir until it coats the onions and is a shade darker, about 1 minute. Pour in the wine and scrape up any brown bits from the bottom of the skillet. Add the broth, beans, tomatoes, and oregano. Bring to a boil. Add the chicken to the skillet along with any juices from the plate. Cook until the chicken is done.

Stir the cheese into the bean mixture and season with salt and pepper. Serve with noodles or rice, using extra Parmesan cheese for topping. You may want to garnish with fresh oregano.

TO FREEZE DRY: Use presets to freeze dry.

TO REHYDRATE: For every 1 ounce of Spicy Chicken Thighs, add 3 ounces of boiling water. Add more as needed.

Stir well, cover, and let sit 15 minutes. Check occasionally to stir and add more water if needed.

INGREDIENTS

2½ lbs	**Boneless/skinless chicken thighs**
	Kosher salt and freshly ground pepper
3 Tbsp.	**Extra virgin olive oil**
1 small	**Onion, chopped**
4 cloves	**Garlic, finely chopped**
¼ tsp. (or to taste)	**Red pepper flakes**
1 Tbsp.	**Tomato paste**
½ cup	**Dry white wine**
2 cups	**Chicken broth**
1 can (15 oz.)	**Cannellini beans, rinsed and drained**
1 can (14 oz.)	**Diced tomatoes**
1 tsp.	**Dried oregano**
⅓ cup	**Grated Parmesan**

Optional: fresh oregano (for garnish)

Magic Meatballs *(Kim Kane)*

INSTRUCTIONS:

In a large non-stick skillet, heat 2 tablespoons of olive oil, add the chopped onions, and cook until soft, about 3 minutes. Season with a pinch of salt and pepper and transfer to a bowl with bread crumbs.

Add the ground meat, milk, egg, parsley, salt, and spices to the bread crumbs and onions. Mix well to combine.

From the meat mixture, make as many 1/2" meatballs as the recipe allows. Do not pack these too tightly as it makes them hard to rehydrate. Set aside on a plate.

Heat oil and butter in a skillet over medium-high heat. Brown the meatballs on all sides.

Pour the broth into the skillet and bring to a boil, stirring to scrape the browned bits up from the bottom of the skillet.

Stir in the cream of mushroom soup and the sour cream and worcestershire sauce.

Serve the meatballs while they are hot with noodles, pouring over the sauce and sprinkling fresh parsley on top.

INGREDIENTS

½ cup	**Bread crumbs**
1	**Small onion**
2 Tbsp.	**Olive oil**
1 Tbsp.	**Fresh parsley, finely chopped**
1 lb.	**Lean ground beef**
½ lb.	**Lean ground pork**
¼ cup	**Milk**
1	**Egg**
¼ tsp.	**Ground nutmeg**
⅛ tsp.	**Ground allspice**
½ tsp.	**Garlic powder or granulated garlic**
1 tsp.	**Kosher salt**
¼ tsp.	**Ground black pepper**

For Frying Meatballs:

1 Tbsp.	**Olive oil**
2 Tbsp.	**Butter**

For Mushroom Soup Sauce:

1 cup	**Beef broth**
2 cans	**Cream of mushroom soup**
¼ cup	**Sour cream**
1 Tbsp.	**Worcestershire sauce**

TO FREEZE DRY:

Place the sauce on one tray and the meatballs on another.

(Note: You can freeze dry the meatballs and sauce together, but it's difficult to get the meatballs to rehydrate without making the sauce too soupy.)

TO REHYDRATE:

Place the meatballs in a container with a lid. Pour enough boiling water to cover and place on the lid. Let sit for 10 minutes while checking occasionally. Drain when done.

For every 1 ounce of sauce, start with 3 ounces of boiling water, adding it slowly while whisking. Continue to add more water until the sauce is the consistency you prefer.

Seasoned Indian White Beans (Kim Kane)

This can be served as a side dish, or add diced lean ham for a main dish.

INSTRUCTIONS:

Heat oil in a skillet and fry the onion till golden brown. Add the sliced garlic and fry for a few seconds before adding the chopped ginger. Let it sizzle before adding the chopped tomato. Stir everything until the pieces of tomato soften.

Reduce the heat and add the chilli powder, turmeric powder, and chaat masala. Fry everything well. Add the beans, then salt and pepper to taste.

TO FREEZE DRY: Freeze dry as normal.

TO REHYDRATE: For every 1 ounce of Seasoned White beans, add 3 ounces of boiling water.

Stir well, cover, and let sit 15 minutes. Check occasionally to stir and add more water if needed.

INGREDIENTS

2 cans	**White beans, drained**
1 medium	**Onion, finely sliced**
2-3 cloves	**Garlic, sliced horizontally**
1 inch	**Ginger, chopped**
1 medium	**Tomato, roughly chopped**
1 tsp.	**Red chili powder, to taste**
½ tsp.	**Turmeric powder**
½ tsp.	**Chaat masala powder**

Oil for frying

Chopped coriander to garnish

Grapes (John Meyer)

I have received great reviews on these freeze-dried grapes. They maintain their shape without wrinkles. Also, you can squeeze them between your fingers and they crumble.

INSTRUCTIONS:

Bring a pot of water to boil. Add grapes. As water returns to a boil, the grapes will begin to float.

Scoop them out as they float to the top, and put them in a bowl of ice water to cool quickly. Freeze until solid, then run in freeze dryer.

Tuna Salad (John Meyer)

This recipe will fill two medium freeze dryer trays.

INSTRUCTIONS:

Add tuna (with the water included) to the softened cheese. Mix in onions, celery, and relish. Spread on two medium freeze dryer trays and place in freezer until frozen solid. Transfer to pre-frozen freeze dryer.

INGREDIENTS

2 (8 oz.) pkgs.	**Softened cream cheese**
2 (12 oz.)	**Cans tuna in water, undrained**
1 cup	**Chopped onions**
1 cup	**Finely chopped celery**
1 cup	**Sweet pickle relish**

TO REHYDRATE:

Be very careful while adding water. It doesn't take much, so work in small amounts until you are happy with the consistency. Enjoy.

Freeze-Dried Mayo Substitute (John Meyer)

Option: use modular molds to freeze dry as individual servings.

INSTRUCTIONS:

Mix all ingredients well and freeze dry. It powders easily. Use modular molds to make individual servings. Seal finished product in Mylar bags or jars with appropriately sized oxygen absorber.

INGREDIENTS

1 (8 oz.) pkg.	**Softened cream cheese**
1½ tsp.	**Lemon juice**
1 tsp.	**Vinegar**
¼ tsp.	**Mustard**
½ tsp.	**Salt**
¼ cup	**2% milk**

TO REHYDRATE:

Remove desired amount from package, and add small amounts of water to rehydrate for use.

Watch a video tutorial about preparation and use on YouTube at John in Bibs, episodes 59 and 60.

Potato Salad *(John Meyer)*

This recipe will fill four medium freeze dryer trays.

INSTRUCTIONS:

Mix cream cheese and pickle juice together until you have a smooth consistency. Add chopped celery and onion, stirring together well. Add relish and mustard. Mix well. Add potatoes, stirring until everything is well coated.

This recipe will fill 4 medium freeze dryer trays. After the cycle is complete, package in Mylar bags, add appropriate oxygen absorber, and seal.

TO REHYDRATE:

Remove desired amount of freeze-dried potato salad from Mylar bag. Add water slowly, stirring until desired consistency is obtained. Enjoy!

INGREDIENTS

5 lbs.	**Peeled potatoes, diced and cooked**
2 (8 oz.) pkgs.	**Softened cream cheese**
½ cup	**Bread & butter pickle juice**
2 cups	**Chopped celery**
2 cups	**Chopped onion**
1 cup	**Sweet relish**
3 Tbsp.	**Yellow mustard (could add more or less depending on your preference)**

Season with celery seed, salt, and pepper to taste

Watch a video tutorial on YouTube at John in Bibs, episode 57.

146

Cowboy Caviar (Brian Witmer)

This make 8 cups or enough for 1.25 large freeze dryer trays (4x this recipe for full large load).

INSTRUCTIONS:

In a large mixing bowl, add drained beans, corn, and tomatoes.

Dice avocado, onion, pepper, jalapeño, and cilantro. Add to bowl.

Add chili powder, cumin, and lime juice, then salt and pepper to taste.

Mix all ingredients.

You can also freeze dry tortilla shells to make chips (try spritzing them with lime juice).

TO REHYDRATE:

Add water to preferred consistency and let sit for 5 minutes.

INGREDIENTS

(fresh ingredients can be substituted for canned at 15 oz. each)

1 can	**Black beans**
1 can	**Black eyed peas**
1 can	**Diced tomatoes (we like Rotel for some spice)**
1 can	**Corn**
1	**Avocado**
1	**Onion**
1	**Red or orange bell pepper**
1	**Jalapeño**
	Fresh cilantro
1 tsp.	**Chili powder**
1 tsp.	**Cumin**
	Salt and pepper
¼ cup	**Lime juice**

Find more tips and recipes on Facebook at 'Retired at 40-Live. Life. Simple.'

Smoked Mac & Cheese *(Donna Hoaks)*

INSTRUCTIONS:

Place sauce ingredients in a crock-pot on high.

Let the sauce heat for about an hour. You should be able to stir it, and it should start looking like sauce. It doesn't have to be completely melted together since the heat from the pasta will finish the process.

Cook 2 pounds of elbow or shell pasta in a large pot according to package directions. Drain, reserving 3 cups of pasta water.

NOTE: If you are making this ahead of time to reheat later in the oven, cook till firm but not done. About half-cooked and pliable but not al dente.

Put pasta back in large pot and add sauce, stirring to melt the sauce into the pasta. If it is too stiff, add some of the reserved water to thin a bit. Stir in liquid smoke and ground cumin. Taste and add more smoke and cumin if you desire a heavier smoke flavor.

INGREDIENTS

Sauce:

8 oz.	**Cream cheese**
1 stick	**Real butter**
1 can	**Evaporated milk**
16 oz.	**Velveeta, cubed**
8 oz.	**Extra sharp cheddar**

Additional Ingredients:

2 lbs.	**Elbow or shell pasta**
¼ cup or to taste	**Liquid smoke**
2 Tbsp.	**Ground cumin**

If you are serving later, place in a foil pan, cover, and cool in the refrigerator. Reheat in a 350°F oven for 1 hour. The pasta should finish cooking and be perfect.

TO FREEZE DRY: Freeze dry as normal.

TO REHYDRATE. Rehydrate with boiling water, adding a little at a time as needed. This dish needs a little time to rehydrate, and it's worth it. Though there are lots of fats in the sauce, the freeze-dried product is perfect, and it stores well.

Grandpa Halls' Almost Famous Baked Beans

(Brent Halls, Inventor of the Harvey Filter)

You will need at least an 8-quart cooking pot. This recipe will make a little less than that and will fill four trays in the medium-sized freeze dryer, with a little extra to sample first.

INSTRUCTIONS:

Sauté the onions and peppers in the butter until soft. Add all remaining ingredients (except the beans and ham). Heat well while stirring to dissolve the sugar.

Add the beans and ham and bring back to temperature. You don't need to simmer or boil, just heat to let the flavors blend.

Taste it. If it's good, it's ready!

Bacon that's already been cooked is also great in this recipe. Or, use pulled pork (cut in smaller pieces first), sausage, hamburger, or no meat at all.

TO FREEZE DRY: Ladle the beans by cups onto the trays (each tray in the medium-size freeze dryer holds about 6 cups).

When the cycle is complete, crumble and package as you normally would. Enjoy!

INGREDIENTS

2 Tbsp.	**Butter**
2 medium	**Yellow onions, chopped**
2 pkgs.	**Kroger "Recipe Beginnings" pepper and onion blend (you could also make these from scratch). Chop or break into smaller pieces while frozen.**
2-3 cups	**Brown sugar (use 3 cups if you like your beans sweet)**
3 cups	**Ketchup**
1 jar (12 oz.)	**Heinz chili sauce**
2 cups	**Bbq sauce**
2 Tbsp.	**Yellow mustard**
8 cans	**(16.5 oz.) Bush's baked beans**
3 cups	**Ham, finely trimmed and cut into about 1" square by 1/4" thick pieces.**

Optional: Hot sauce or crushed red pepper to taste

Cheesy Chili Mac (Brian Witmer)

This recipe will fill two-trays worth in a large freeze dryer (approximately 9 cups).

INSTRUCTIONS:

Put a few tablespoons of broth at the bottom of a large pot or large frying pan.

Add garlic and chopped onion. Cook for a few minutes, add the bell pepper, and cook until onions are translucent.

In a separate pan, cook lean ground beef and cook until browned (drain, rinse, and towel to remove as much oil as possible).

Take heat up to high and add ground beef back into the first frying pan. Mix together.

Add in crushed tomatoes and remaining broth.

Add in drained kidney beans and macaroni.

Add in spices and take heat down to medium for 10-12 minutes or until macaroni is cooked but still firm.

Sauce should be thick, not watery. Add cheese if desired.

TO REHYDRATE: Rehydration for 3.9 oz. serving: add 1½ cups boiling water, let sit for 5 minutes, stir and let sit for an additional 5 minutes.

INGREDIENTS

2 cloves	**Garlic, minced**
1	**Onion, chopped**
1	**Bell pepper**
1 lb.	**Lean ground beef**
1 can (28 oz.)	**Crushed tomatoes**
15 oz. can	**Kidney beans**
2 ¾ cup	**Broth (we like vegetable)**
8 oz.	**Elbow macaroni**
1 tsp.	**Cayenne pepper**
2 tsp.	**Paprika**
2 tsp.	**Cumin**
1½ tsp.	**Onion or garlic powder**
1 tsp.	**Oregano**
½ tsp.	**Pepper**
To taste	**Salt**

Optional: Top with the cheese of your preference

Cereal Bars (Brian Witmer)

Use your favorite cereal and mix in some additional ingredients for an easy homemade treat!

INSTRUCTIONS:

Start by putting your extra ingredients on the bottom layer, like strawberries or blueberries.

Put cereal on top of that (filling trays about halfway up the sides).

Spread enough on trays to make layers of ingredients. Place trays into unit, then slide out tray partway to add regular or chocolate milk as your glue (it holds everything together).

You don't need to fill the trays to the top. Just cover the cereal, but make sure there is enough to hold the bar together once it's freeze dried.

After freeze drying, use a knife to cut, or use tray dividers when assembling before freeze drying to form portions.

TO REHYDRATE:

Bars can be rehydrated as a bowl of cereal. Add water in small portions until cereal reaches desired consistency.

INGREDIENTS

Favorite cereal

Regular milk or chocolate milk

Extra ingredients like flaxseed, raisins, strawberries, blueberries, or PB2

Food Tips From Our Fans

FRUITS (Kim Kane)

If the fruit is sour going into the freeze dryer, it will be sour coming out. Adding a hint of sugar before freeze drying helps.

APPLES (Kim Kane)

Apples can be freeze dried with or without skins. If you plan to rehydrate the apples for use in cooking, it might be best to remove the skins.

To freeze dry, slice, keeping them even and under ½" (peeling optional). Place in a bowl of cool water with a bit of lemon to keep them from browning as you work. Once sliced, arrange on your trays. They do not stick to the trays but they will stick to each other, just slightly, but are easy to break apart.

Sprinkling cinnamon or cinnamon sugar on them is amazing. You can also powder other fruits like berries or bananas and sprinkle that powder on them for fun, interesting treats.

Rehydration for cooking:
Place in enough cool water to cover and let sit for 5 minutes, giving them an occasional stir. Once done, use as called for in your recipe.

POTATOES (Kim Kane)

Note: Raw potatoes must be blanched before freeze drying or they will turn black. Fresh diced potatoes should be blanched for about 4 minutes, shredded should be blanched for 2 minutes. Then place in an ice bath to stop the cooking.

POTATO CHUNKS:

Mix 1/2 cup of freeze-dried potato chunks (approx. ½" size) with 1 cup of hot water. Let the potatoes sit, covered, until rehydrated. Then you can fry, mash or bake like normal. If you are using in a soup, just toss them in and let them cook with the other ingredients.

APPLESAUCE (Kim Kane)

Store-bought or homemade applesauce does very well in the freeze dryer. Simply fill your trays, ensuring you do not exceed the weight limit for your machine and that's it. The sauce might stick a little so you might choose to use parchment paper or silicone mats. Depending on the amount of sugar in the sauce the final product might vary. Low sugar powders better. Higher sugar content comes out kind of "bendy." Either is fine.

Rehydration:
For every 1 ounce of applesauce, use 2 ounces of cool water to start. Stir, and when it reaches the consistency you like you're done. If not keep slowly adding the water until it is the right consistency. It's that simple.

SUMMER SQUASH (Kim Kane)

We recommend removing the skin from summer squash unless you're going to shred it. You can prepare the squash several different ways:

CUBED:

Peel, then cut into ½" squares and place on trays.

To rehydrate, cover in boiling water and let sit covered for 5 minutes.

Add more time as needed. These can be used in soups, stews, breaded and fried, or just sauteed in butter.

SLICED:

Peel, then cut into ¼" slices and place on trays. Can be used to replace noodles in things like lasagna. You can freeze dry them in noodle form but they are really delicate.

SHREDDED!

To rehydrate shredded summer squash, place squash in a colander and spray warm water on while gently stirring. They only take a minute or two to rehydrate. Then pat dry with a paper towel. These can be used for breads, cakes, stir fry, and our favorite, zucchini fritters (see page 123).

Freeze Dryer Tips From Our Fans

- Place trays into freeze dryer and then pull out slightly to fill with liquids. Or, place in the freezer and pour in liquids to pre-freeze.

- Stack trays in the freezer using plastic dividers or tray lids.

- Use parchment paper or silicone mats (especially for food that sticks after being freeze dried).

- Use mesh or parchment paper with slices cut into it so you can stack food on trays.

- Write on Mylar bags before filling them with food.

- Freeze foods such as puddings and yogurts in silicone molds.

- Meals can be rehydrated directly in the packaging, a large cup, bowl, or pot. Water does not need to be boiling, just hot enough to rehydrate efficiently. The cooler the water, the longer it may take to rehydrate.

  To rehydrate: cover food with warm, not necessarily boiling, water. The amount of water will vary depending on the freeze-dried food and whether you want a soupy or thicker food.

Remember, it's easy to add water if there isn't enough, but it's difficult to remove water. Most food will rehydrate in 10-15 minutes.

Chapter 9

Freeze-Dried Candy and Snacks

Freeze-Dried Candy and Snacks

Place on parchment paper or silicone mats to prevent sticking to trays.

Saltwater Taffy

INSTRUCTIONS:

Cut in half or thirds and place on trays, leaving space that approximates the diameter of each piece since they puff up and expand. Freeze dry.

Ice Cream Sandwich Bites

INSTRUCTIONS:

Make sure to pre-freeze the freeze dryer. It's also good to freeze trays beforehand so they are very cold. Slice sandwiches into bite-size pieces, place on tray, re-freeze, then freeze dry.

Ice Cream Scoops

INSTRUCTIONS:

Make sure to pre-freeze the freeze dryer. It's also good to freeze trays beforehand so they are very cold. Take small scoops of ice cream and place on trays, re-freeze, then freeze dry.

Skittles®

INSTRUCTIONS:

Place on trays in a single layer with a little spacing between each to allow for expansion (otherwise, they might stick to each other).

Cheesecake Bites

INSTRUCTIONS:

Make your own or purchase your favorite cheesecake. Place it in your freezer until it is frozen. Once it's frozen, cut the cheesecake into bite-size pieces and place them in the freeze dryer.

Gummy Bears

INSTRUCTIONS:

Be sure to leave quite a bit of space between each bear as they usually double in size by the time they are freeze dried. Some brands work better than others.

Gummy Worms

INSTRUCTIONS:

Place on trays with plenty of space in between each gummy worm. They will puff up several times their original size. (Image shows non-freeze-dried gummy worm on the left.)

Milk Duds®

INSTRUCTIONS:

Place on tray, spaced out. If they don't freeze dry well, try cutting in half.

Marshmallows

INSTRUCTIONS:

Spread on trays. Mini marshmallows can be left whole; for larger marshmallows, consider cutting into thirds or quarters.

Caramels

INSTRUCTIONS:

Cut store-bought chewy caramels in half (they puff) and place on trays, leaving space for expansion.

Many candies can be freeze dried, so have fun experimenting with different ones. Even different brands of the same candy can have different results.

Yogurt Drops

INSTRUCTIONS:

Yogurt brands with more sugar hold their shape better. Greek yogurt doesn't freeze dry as well and it powders.

Line your tray with parchment paper or a silicone mat. Use a plastic bag or cake decorator bag to put small dollops of yogurt on a freeze dryer tray. Once freeze dried, they can be placed in an airtight jar on the kitchen counter and eaten by the handful.

Crunchy Jell-O Snacks

INSTRUCTIONS:

Whisk all ingredients in a 13×9 pan or mix and pour into silicone molds. Refrigerate until firm. If using a pan, dip the bottom of it in warm water before cutting. Cut the Jell-O into cubes, place the cubes on a freeze dryer tray lined with a silicone mat or parchment paper and freeze dry. Enjoy them as a crunchy snack.

INGREDIENTS

3 small boxes	**Jell-O, your favorite flavor**
4 envelopes	**Knox unflavored gelatin**
4 cups	**Boiling water**

Whipped Cream Dollops

INSTRUCTIONS:

Freeze-dried whipped cream dollops are perfect for adding to hot chocolate or other hot drinks with added cream. Line trays with silicone or parchment paper, then spray or dollop the cream onto pre-frozen trays, leaving space between each dollop. Freeze again before loading into pre-frozen freeze dryer.

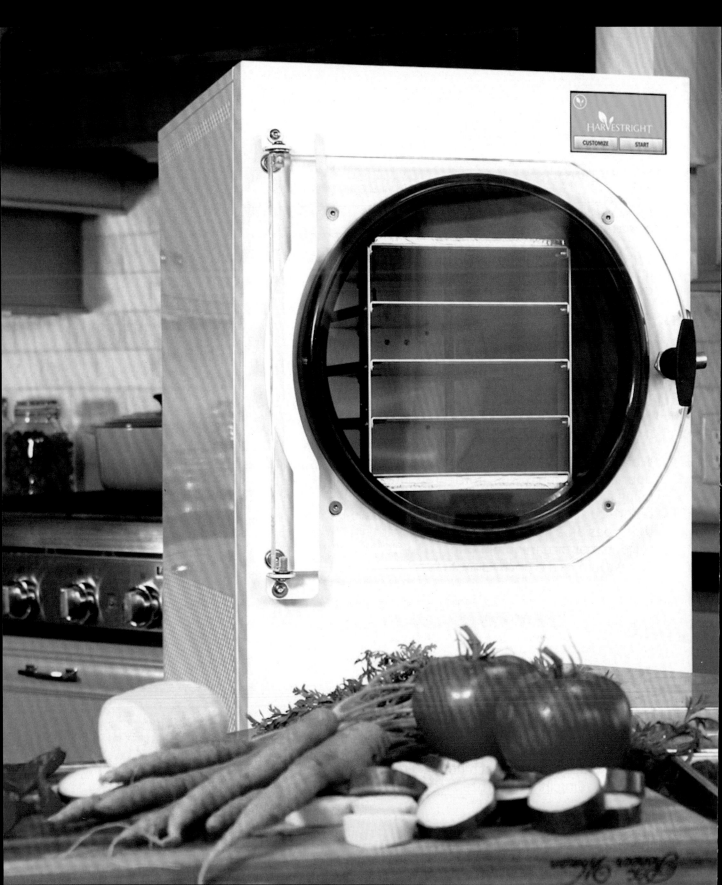

Chapter 10
Caring For Your Freeze Dryer

Maintenance

Taking good care of your freeze dryer ensures you will benefit from this amazing machine for years to come!

TIP: Check the pump's oil level before each use.

If your freeze dryer has an oil vacuum pump attached, the pump has a gauge on the front indicating the oil level. Use the gauge to make sure the oil level isn't too high or too low.

 Look at the oil through the sight glass. If it isn't clear, change it.

 It's easier to drain oil when the vacuum pump is still hot.

CLEAN OIL

CLOUDY OIL - NEEDS CHANGING

OIL IS TOO DIRTY: DON'T ALLOW

Defrost and drain the machine after every batch.

Ice will build up on the inner walls of the freeze dryer after each batch. Remove your freeze-dried food and get rid of the ice by closing the door and running a "Defrost" cycle.

Before you do so, make sure that the drain tube coming from the back of the freeze dryer is placed in a sink or a bucket and that the drain valve is open.

If you have time between cycles, you can leave the door open and the unit will defrost itself.

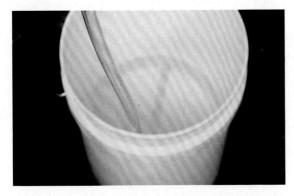

Make sure that the drain tube is placed in a sink or a bucket and that the drain valve is open.

After every batch, be sure to empty your container or bucket that the water has drained into. Otherwise, when you open your drain valve to release the pressure in the freeze dry chamber at the end of the batch, the water in your bucket can get pulled into your food chamber. This will destroy the food that you freeze dried.

TIP: Leave the door unlatched when it's not in use to avoid mold forming from any moisture remaining in the freeze dryer.

Cleaning Instructions

Vacuum Chamber & Shelves:

First, unplug your freeze dryer from the wall. Clean the vacuum chamber and shelves with a mild detergent and wipe dry with a soft cloth.

Remove shelves for a thorough cleaning. In order to remove the shelves, you will need to take off the black rubber gasket that seals the door. Gently pull out the shelf, then disconnect the cable. Once the red tab is unlocked, press the black tab down and pull the two pieces apart. When you're finished cleaning, ensure that the shelves and chamber are dry. Next, reconnect the power line to the shelving unit.

It is important to clean the chamber and the shelf on a regular basis. It is necessary to do this by hand. You can put the shelf in a large sink and wash it with dish soap, brushes, and rags. Don't use a dishwasher because it can get so hot, it will melt the glue and cause the heating pads to fall off.

Shelf unit being removed.

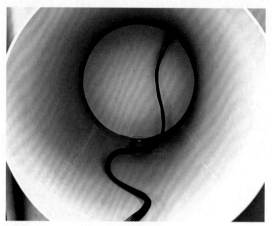

Empty vacuum chamber showing the shelf cable after shelf removal.

 Using a dishwasher to wash the shelf unit will void the freeze dryer warranty.

Exterior:

The outer door, handle, and cabinet surfaces should be cleaned with warm water and a mild detergent, then wiped dry with a soft cloth.

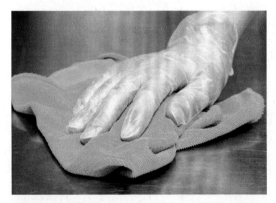

Wipe down surfaces with warm water and mild detergent using a soft cloth.

Door gasket can be washed with mild soap and water.

Bad Odors? Freeze dry tomato sauce or cooked rice to get rid of odd odors. Or, just leave the door open overnight.

Cleaning Cautions:

Do not use stiff-bristled brushes or abrasive cloths or pads to clean the inside or outside of the freeze dryer as this will dull or scratch the surface.

NO BENZENE PAINT THINNER BLEACH

Do not use benzene, paint thinner, or Clorox for cleaning. They may damage the surface of the appliance and can even cause fires.

Troubleshooting Tips

- Make sure the black rubber gasket that attaches to the front of the chamber is clean and free from debris.

- Make sure the hose attachment is tight and the O-Ring inside the hose is good.

- Make sure vacuum pump is plugged into the back of the unit with the power switch turned on.

- To get a better seal, slightly pull out the black rubber gasket before closing the door.

- Make sure the tray unit is inserted, with the orange side on the bottom.

- Drain the oil from the pump if it's not going to be used for an extended period of time.

- If you aren't using the freeze dryer for an extended period of time, be sure to leave the door open to avoid any mold.

Be sure to turn the handle all the way until the door completely latches.

Make sure the door is clean and free from debris.

Make sure the drain valve is turned completely and closed. If it's loose, simple tighten the screw with a Phillips screwdriver.

Additional Questions?
Visit HarvestRight.com/support

Index

Recipe Index

CREDITS